KEVIN KACHIN
NICK PROPPER

STRESSED SELF TO BEST SELF

THE SCIENCE-BACKED SYSTEM FOR SUSTAINABLE PEAK PERFORMANCE

WILEY

Published by John Wiley & Sons, Inc., Hoboken, New Jersey.

Library of Congress Cataloging-in-Publication Data:

Names: Kachin, Kevin author | Propper, Nick author
Title: Stressed self to best self : the science-backed system for sustainable peak performance / Kevin Kachin, PhD, and Nick Propper.
Description: Hoboken, New Jersey : Wiley, [2026] | Includes bibliographical references and index.
Identifiers: LCCN 2026019643 (print) | LCCN 2026019644 (ebook) | ISBN 9781394421541 hardback | ISBN 9781394421565 adobe pdf | ISBN 9781394421558 epub
Subjects: LCSH: Stress (Psychology) | Burn out (Psychology) | Burn out (Psychology)—Prevention
Classification: LCC BF575.S75 K33 2026 (print) | LCC BF575.S75 (ebook)
LC record available at https://lccn.loc.gov/2026019643
LC ebook record available at https://lccn.loc.gov/2026019644

Cover Design: Paul McCarthy
Cover Art: © Miragec/Getty Images
Author Photos: Eric Campbell and Heidi Curran
Printed and bound by CPI Group (UK) Ltd, Croydon, CR0 4YY

C9781394421541_110826

Healthcare Disclaimer

THIS BOOK IS intended for educational and informational purposes only and does not provide medical advice or professional healthcare services. The information presented should not be used for diagnosing or treating any health condition. Readers should always seek medical advice from a qualified healthcare provider regarding any medical concerns.

Never disregard professional medical advice or delay seeking it due to information found in this book. No physician-patient relationship is created by the use of this book. Neither the publisher nor the authors make any express or implied representations regarding the use of the information contained herein.

This book may appear in various formats, including electronic and print versions. Some content available in print may not be included in electronic formats, and vice versa.

To you, the reader, for choosing to engage in the concepts and strategies provided in this book.

As you apply what you learn, your mind, body, and loved ones will thank you for improving both your quality of life. . . and theirs.

Contents

Preface		*ix*
Introduction: The Two Versions of You		*xi*
Part I	**Awareness**	**1**
Chapter 1	Making the Invisible Visible	3
Chapter 2	What Happens When You're Stressed?	5
Chapter 3	Recognizing Your Stressed Self in Action	23
Chapter 4	Your Gateway to Change	33
Chapter 5	Meeting and Unlocking Your Best Self	43
Chapter 6	Barriers to Being Your Best Self	53
Chapter 7	Regulating Your Emotions	57
Chapter 8	Defining Intentional Recovery	77

Part II	**Strategies**	**87**
Chapter 9	A New Way Forward	89
Chapter 10	Moving to Thrive	93
Chapter 11	Hydrating Your Way to Increased Energy	113
Chapter 12	Breathing Your Way to Calm and Focused	123
Chapter 13	Sleeping Your Way to the Safety Signal	135
Chapter 14	Managing Stressors	149
Chapter 15	Narrating Your Way to Your Best	165
Part III	**Action**	**177**
Chapter 16	Planning Intentional Recovery	179
Chapter 17	Clarifying Your Micro Mission	183
Chapter 18	Impactful Growth Plan	185
Chapter 19	Your Environment	191
Conclusion: Live It Forward		*197*
References		*199*
Acknowledgments		*215*
About the Authors		*217*
Index		*219*

Preface

PICTURE YOURSELF IN two very distinct states that are on opposite sides of the well-being and performance spectrum.

On one side, there is a version of you that is full of energy, drive, and purpose. Each day, you wake up feeling focused, grounded, and ready for what lies ahead. Let's call this version your **Best Self**, the version that you aspire to be.

Now, imagine the exact opposite. A version of you that constantly feels tense, worried, and irritable. You rush through your speech and actions, your thoughts are scattered, and your patience is thin. Even the smallest challenges overwhelm you. This is your **Stressed Self**, the version that often takes over when life feels too demanding.

The reality is that all of us shift between these two versions of ourselves all the time. When stress is left unmanaged, your Stressed Self might show up more often than you would like, affecting your relationships, performance, and overall well-being. If you are like many people we train, you may have never actually met your Best Self.

This book is all about helping you recognize and understand both of these versions of yourself. Neither state is inherently wrong, and even stress can have its benefits. The key is becoming aware of when you are in which state and learning how to effectively pause in order to shift between them. By understanding the tools and wisdom needed to move from stress to balance, your Best Self can emerge more often. The more frequently your Best Self emerges, the more you are training that version of you. Eventually that version becomes your default.

This process all starts by learning how to effectively pause. Intellectually, it is a simple process to understand. Consistent implementation of intentional pauses is the challenge that you will overcome through your learning from this book.

Similar to our training programs, we have structured the book into three parts: Awareness, Strategies, and Action. You may have the urge to skip directly to the Strategies part as that is what you are here to learn. We advise against doing that. Unlike other books that give you the option to start from anywhere in the text, we advise that you read this book linearly, as each chapter builds from the previous chapters. For example, you need to read the Part 1 chapters on awareness before the Part 2 chapters on strategies because, as we often tell our training participants, "awareness is the most important strategy." If you are not aware of when you are experiencing stress, it does not matter how many strategies you know or how effective they may be; without being aware that you are experiencing stress, you will not know when to implement them.

Introduction: The Two Versions of You

STRESS IS NO longer just the pressure of a looming deadline or a difficult conversation. For many, it has become the constant background of life, a chronic and unrelenting force that shapes how we think, feel, relate, and show up in the world.

It's no surprise then that chronic stress has a deep ripple effect across every area of your life. Physically, it drains your energy, compromises your immune system, and disrupts sleep, promoting inflammation and increasing the risk of serious conditions such as heart disease, obesity, and diabetes.[1,2] Emotionally, it lowers your resilience and leaves you feeling more reactive and overwhelmed. Mentally, it narrows your focus and impairs your ability to think clearly or make sound decisions. Relationally, it reduces empathy and patience, leading to more conflict, distance, or disconnection with yourself and those you care about most. Over time, chronic stress can lead to burnout—a state of total exhaustion that impacts every area of your life.[3,4]

Even your sense of purpose or meaning can be affected when chronic stress pulls you into survival mode. When your nervous system is on high alert, it becomes harder to access the parts of you that are creative, open, connected, and resourceful. And these are typically the characteristics you rely on the most throughout the day to perform at your desired level. Not just in your work life, but also in terms of how you perform for the people and things that are waiting for you when you step away from the work.

No wonder, then, that 71% of adults in a national survey reported at least one symptom of stress in the past month and almost half said it keeps them awake at night.[5] Also at an economic level, stress is quietly taking its toll. Gallup estimates that chronic workplace stress costs global businesses more than $480 billion every year through lost productivity, absenteeism, turnover, and medical expenses.[6,7]

Yet despite its widespread impact, stress is often minimized and treated as a personal weakness or simply a fact of life to be endured. Society seems to celebrate those who seem to manage everything—careers, families, personal growth—without recognizing the inner strain or the emotional toll that being an "always-on" high performer takes on a person physically, emotionally, and mentally. And we often simply assume that these people are built differently to us and believe that we'll never be able to replicate that level of performance ourselves.

How does this happen?

It happens because most people are never taught how to become aware of and release stress in a meaningful way. Instead, they rely on coping strategies shaped by habit, survival, or urgency, ways of functioning that may help in the short term but often reinforce deeper exhaustion in the long run.

Expecting someone to manage stress without proper knowledge and tools is like asking them to drive a car in a busy city after a few trial runs in an empty parking lot. It's possible, but far from effective and often dangerous over time. Avoiding stress is not a neutral choice. It's an unconscious decision to accept the consequences. From our perspective at Impact Human Performance (IHP), the price is too high to gamble with because that price is almost always paid by your body, mind, and relationships. Just because you are still somehow functioning right now does not mean you are healthy. . .or will remain so in the future.

The truth is, stress rarely announces itself dramatically. It shows up quietly in blurry thoughts during meetings, that annoying ache that persists daily, mental absence over dinner, or the relentless pressure of unfinished tasks circling your mind at 3 a.m. It leaves you drained, reactive and disconnected from the people and goals that matter most. You may be experiencing some of this right now. Otherwise, you probably wouldn't be holding this book.

What If There Was Another Way?

Yes, you read that right. What if there was another way for you, your organization, and your employees? What if there was a different truth? What if you could stay productive, effective, and successful without constantly feeling stressed or overwhelmed? And what if those who aren't burned out yet could be given the tools to manage their energy and stress in a truly effective and sustainable way? And what if the energy, growth, and purpose could actually be restored for those who are already feeling drained every day?

We believe in this different way. We believe individuals can be empowered to recover more effectively from stress, optimize their energy, and deepen their sense of purpose, all while strengthening their human connections. With more than 30 years of combined experience, we do not make this claim lightly. United in our mission to develop and facilitate programs on stress, recovery, and impactful leadership, we formed IHP in 2021. Since then, we have trained hundreds of thousands of people across the United States Military, United States Federal Government, and Fortune 500 companies. Our solutions are grounded in the latest research in neuroscience, psychophysiology, performance psychology, and leadership development.

Today, more than 150,000 employees have daily access to our training solutions. With this book, we are sharing our signature program on stress and recovery so you can learn and train on your own, share it with your team, or even implement it across your entire organization.

We believe this content should be accessible to everyone. That's why this book is not only filled with the practical knowledge and easy to understand science behind stress management and recovery, but is also designed as an interactive workbook that you can personalize. Through guided practices, deep reflections, and personal commitments, you will have the tools to integrate these powerful concepts into your daily life.

Who Is This Book for, and How to Use It?

This book is for busy professionals who want to stay up to date with the latest science in understanding and managing stress so they can navigate this constant companion effectively while still performing at their best. It is also for those who feel they are not at their best right now and are looking for practical, science-based guidance to regain balance and get back to being at their best, more often. Most importantly, it is for those of you who are so drained that you are experiencing life detached from yourself and others: on the outside you are completing your obligations, but inside it feels as though something is "broken" in your brain and with little/no charge remaining on your human energy battery.

Leaders will benefit by gaining deeper insights and inspiration for sharing these concepts with their teams. Entrepreneurs, whether starting alone or with a small team, will find essential tools to manage stress and recovery, helping to stay focused and effective both when things are flowing and when challenges arise. And employees at any stage of their career will discover valuable strategies for daily life, equipping them with the tools they need to manage said daily life right now, as well as for whatever is coming next.

What Content Can You Expect?

This book will take you on a journey. You will reflect deeply and get to know the two versions of yourself: your Stressed Self and your Best Self. Starting with your Stressed Self, you will gain a deeper understanding of the science of stress, along with its physical, mental, and emotional aspects, helping you to recognize it more easily. Most people don't even realize they are stressed until they reach a point of overwhelm, and only then do they call it stress. The information in this book will change that. By increasing your awareness of stress in general and how it manifests in you, you'll become more attuned to both your own stress and that of others when it starts taking the driver's seat.

We will explore practical actions you can take the moment you notice stress creeping in. And in case you, your team, or your leadership have ever questioned the importance of stress and recovery management, we'll map out exactly what happens when these aspects are ignored.

In Part 1 you will increase your awareness by learning the difference between stress and stressors, which will allow you to become more familiar with who you are when you experience stress (i.e., Stressed Self). Once you've discovered your Stressed Self, we'll guide you on the inspiring journey to uncover your Best Self, that part of you that is ready to step forward as your stress levels decrease. Even if you feel far from your Best Self right now, this section will help you visualize and ignite the motivation to reconnect with it. Finally, we will establish a framework around the concept of emotional regulation that determines which version of yourself you are moving toward at any given moment.

In Part 2 we will dive deeply into the most impactful behaviors that support your ability to move from your Stressed Self to your Best Self. Not only will we cover the essentials of movement, hydration, sleep, and even breathing, but we will also introduce practices and ideas that expand your perspective, helping you to handle stress more skillfully, move through overwhelm with greater ease, and respond to challenges with clarity and strength instead of being consumed by them.

Finally, in Part 3 of the book, you will develop a practical, personalized action plan for you to achieve impactful growth moving forward. The focus here will be on implementing strategies that are personal to you and that you will actually do. In our experience many personal development books and trainings offer a plethora of research-based strategies and tactics that seem extremely effective, but people never implement. The action planning you will learn will ensure that you are moving toward your goal(s) even on the most challenging of days.

Everything we have learned from our collective work spanning 30 years is packed into this book for you to apply to your life and, if applicable, to share within your teams. Neither you nor your employees need to be at the mercy of stress. This book will show you how to take control of your energy, refocus your priorities, and unlock your greatest potential at work and at home.

Throughout this book, you will:

- Gain a clear and simple understanding of how stress works and how it affects your mind, body, and emotions.
- Become aware of your stress "warning signs" and develop strategies to manage your stressors.

- Connect to the vision of your Best Self and identify the barriers that prevent you from operating at your best.
- Learn key behaviors that help you shift from your Stressed Self to your Best Self in an effective and systematic way.
- Discover practical tools that fit into your busy life, helping you reclaim energy and clarity.
- Experience growth by learning to recover from stress intentionally and quickly.
- Engage with real-life examples and deep personal reflection for a meaningful and lasting impact.
- Create a personalized plan for essential and intentional recovery throughout your day.

One Last Important Point Before You Begin

Each chapter contains self-reflection questions and practices designed to help you deepen your understanding. It is important to take the time to pause and think through your answers before moving on to the next section. We strongly recommend writing your reflections in the space provided or, if you prefer, in a notebook or journal.

The simple act of writing down your thoughts, feelings, and experiences not only helps reduce stress but also increases your awareness of your thinking patterns and reactions to different people, places, and situations.[8] The more detail you include in your reflections, the easier it will be for your brain to recognize the patterns and signals that influence your day-to-day life. This awareness will make it much easier to apply the strategies you are about to learn.

If you are someone who values growth and self-improvement, consider creating your own stress and recovery journal. Call it whatever resonates with you. The goal is to deepen your reflections and provide yourself with a valuable tool for self-support. At IHP, we strongly believe in this practice as one of the simplest and most effective ways to take care of yourself and continuously grow.

Let's get started.

PART I
Awareness

"Awareness is the greatest agent for change."

—Eckhart Tolle

1

Making the Invisible Visible

IMAGINE WAKING UP one morning and realizing that the constant hum of tension in your chest, the racing thoughts that pull you from sleep, or the quiet frustration that colors your interactions aren't just "how life is." They're signals—invitations to pause, notice, and choose differently. For years, we've worked with high-performing professionals across corporate, military, and government sectors, and one truth stands out: most people are navigating their days on autopilot, reacting to stress without truly understanding it. But what if the first step to reclaiming your energy, your relationships, and your sense of self wasn't about pushing harder or fixing everything at once? What if it started with simply becoming aware?

This opening section of the book, *Part 1: Awareness*, is dedicated to shining a light on the often invisible dynamics of stress in your life. We'll begin by exploring what stress really is, not as an enemy to defeat, but as a natural response that's been wired into us for survival. You'll learn to distinguish between stressors (the external triggers) and stress (your internal reaction), and why that simple delineation can shift how you approach overwhelming moments. We'll dive into the physiology behind your body's "alarm system," how modern-day "hungry lions" like emails and deadlines keep it activated, and the ways chronic stress sneaks in when recovery is absent.

From there, we'll guide you to recognize your own unique Stressed Self—the version of you that emerges under pressure, with its physical tightness, emotional irritability, or mental fog. Through reflections and exercises, you'll map your personal warning signs, those early whispers from your body that, if ignored, turn into screams. We'll also introduce you to your Best Self, helping you define the qualities that light you up when you're aligned, engaged, and flowing. This isn't about aspiration or perfection; it's about clarity—knowing who you are at your core so you can return there more often.

As we progress, we'll unpack the barriers that keep you from your Best Self, including the reactive patterns that reinforce stress and the emotional loops that drain your energy. You'll explore a practical model for emotional regulation, with its four quadrants—High Performance, Stress Response, Forced Recovery, and Intentional Recovery—to help you assess your state in any moment and make informed choices. Finally, we'll set the stage for true change by defining intentional recovery, the deliberate pauses that recharge your human energy battery and create a sustainable rhythm of oscillation between effort and renewal.

Throughout this section, we'll draw on critical insights from our workshops—real stories from leaders who've dismissed their stress as "not legitimate" or chased achievement only to feel empty. You'll find sidebars with classroom moments that mirror your own experiences, reflection prompts to personalize the concepts, and action steps like posting your stress warning signs or Best Self words as visual reminders. These aren't just ideas; they're tools to build awareness through passive repetition, turning "aha" moments into lasting shifts.

By the end of *Part 1*, you'll have a solid foundation: a deeper familiarity with how stress shows up for you, why it persists, and how awareness opens the door to responding rather than reacting. This isn't about eliminating stress—that's neither possible nor desirable. It's about meeting it with curiosity and compassion, so you can access more of your Best Self in the midst of life's demands. Awareness isn't passive observation; it's the spark that empowers you to live with intention.

2

What Happens When You're Stressed?

STRESS IS NOT just a feeling or something imagined. It is real and often reveals itself through clear and noticeable signs, physically, mentally, and emotionally.[1,2] Whether you actually notice the symptoms in yourself or someone else points them out is another story. Stress shows up differently for everyone, and this chapter is dedicated to understanding your own unique stress responses. What leaves you feeling anxious or depleted might feel like a fun challenge to someone else, which is exactly why learning to recognize your personal warning signs is so important.

Critical Insight from the Classroom

One moment that has stayed with us came from a highly tenured executive assistant during a workshop. She had supported senior leaders for most of her career and was widely seen as calm, capable, and unshakeable. During a reflection exercise on stress

(*continued*)

(*continued*)

warning signs, she grew quiet. Then she said something we've since heard in many forms:

> "I don't think I'm allowed to be stressed. I'm not the one with the big title. I'm not accountable for revenue. I'm just support."

That word—*just*—said everything.

For years, she had dismissed her own stress signals. Tight chest. Poor sleep. Irritability at home. Constant mental load. She told herself that because she wasn't "on the front line" of business performance, her stress wasn't legitimate. Other people, she believed, had a right to feel pressure. She didn't.

But your nervous system does not recognize job titles. It does not rank stress by salary band, seniority, or proximity to the boardroom. It responds to **perceived demand, lack of control, social evaluation, uncertainty, and emotional labor**—all of which are often *extremely* high in support roles.

Role strain is driven less by status and more by factors like workload unpredictability, low decision latitude, and emotional regulation demands. Executive assistants, coordinators, military support staff, and government administrators frequently sit in roles where they must anticipate needs, manage others' emotions, prevent problems, and absorb tension—often without authority to change the conditions creating the stress. That combination is a powerful trigger for chronic stress physiology.

In other words, her body had been living in stress response mode even while her mind kept saying, *"This doesn't count."*

That internal invalidation is where the real cost shows up. When you believe you *shouldn't* be stressed, you're far less likely to recover. You don't take the break. You don't speak up. You don't adjust expectations. You override the warning signs. The stress doesn't disappear—it goes underground, where it continues to affect sleep, mood, focus, and relationships.

We hear this in multiple client settings. The logistics officer who says, "The operators have it harder." The HR manager who says, "At least I'm not in sales." The project coordinator who says, "My job isn't that serious." Yet these are often the people holding complex systems together, constantly managing invisible pressure.

Here's the shift: **stress is not a competition, and it is not earned through rank. It is a physiological response to perceived demand. If you are feeling it, it is real.**

Even with all these unique differences, the purpose of the stress response is universal. It activates when you perceive a situation as negative, unmanageable, or threatening. This is a completely natural and even healthy reaction of the body.

That said, it is important to stop viewing stress as something bad or inherently wrong. Instead, consider it as a powerful response developed over millions of years of human evolution to help us adapt and survive.

A Key Delineation: Stress vs. Stressors

If you are like many of our training participants, you often mix up stress and stressors, using the words as if they are the same thing, but that's a mistake that can become confusing when you are trying to get a handle on what's really going on in your experience.

A stressor is the external event, situation, person, or demand that sets off alarm bells in your system, whether it's a looming deadline at work, a heated argument, or even something as mundane as traffic. Stress, on the other hand, is your body's internal reaction to that trigger: the surge of energy hormones, the increased heart rate, the knot in your stomach, or the racing thoughts that follows.[3,4]

People often confuse them because stressors can feel so immediate and overwhelming that we label the whole experience as "stress," but recognizing the distinction is key—when you learn how to tackle the stressor head-on, you will be able to effectively dial down the stress response before it takes over. That said, zeroing in on eliminating or controlling every stressor can backfire big time, sucking up your energy reserves as you chase after things often beyond your reach, which just ramps up the stress you are feeling in the process. The real game-changer is realizing you've got little to no control over most stressors—they are part of the chaotic world we live in—but you have full control over your response to them, even if it doesn't always feel that way in the heat of the moment.

Critical Insight from the Classroom

In one session with a group of senior leaders, we asked a simple question: "When do you feel fulfilled?" The answers came fast. "When we hit targets." "When the project lands." "When the promotion comes through." Achievement. Milestones. Outcomes.

Then one leader paused and said, almost reluctantly, "The problem is. . . that feeling lasts about a day, at best. Then it's straight onto the next thing."

Heads nodded all around the room.

This is a pattern we see up and down the hierarchy and across multiple industries. High performers are often taught, implicitly or explicitly, to tie fulfillment to achievement. Finish the mission. Close the deal. Get the qualification. Reach the rank. And yes, achievement can bring a surge of positive emotion. But this is often a short-lived dopamine spike, not deep, sustained fulfillment. The brain quickly adapts and what once felt like a big win soon becomes the new normal. The bar moves. The chase resumes.

So people end up in a constant cycle: pressure → achievement → brief high → emptiness → more pressure.

No wonder chaos feels draining. If fulfillment only comes at the finish line, then uncertainty, setbacks, and messy middle phases feel like wasted time rather than part of the experience.

In one workshop, a participant reframed this in a powerful way. He said, "The only time I actually feel steady is when I know I'm getting a little better at something, even if everything else is unpredictable."

That's the shift.

Mastery and *growth* as core drivers of lasting fulfillment. When you experience progress—even small, incremental progress—your brain registers competence, agency, and meaning. This taps into deeper psychological needs than achievement alone.

When growth is happening across multiple dimensions—your career, a skill you're learning, your physical health, a relationship you're investing in, a hobby that stretches you—fulfillment becomes less dependent on any single outcome. A tough week at work doesn't wipe you out emotionally if you still feel you're growing as a parent, a partner, a learner, or an athlete. Your sense of progress becomes diversified.

This is where something powerful happens: **you begin to find fulfillment inside the chaos, not after it.**

Uncertainty becomes less threatening because you're no longer measuring your life only by results. You're measuring it by who you are becoming through the process. Challenges shift from being interruptions to being part of the growth environment. Your nervous system still responds to stressors, but your overall experience carries more purpose and meaning in the daily grind.

This leads to a quiet confidence that says, "Even when this is messy, I'm still moving forward somewhere." And that ability to anchor fulfillment in ongoing growth, rather than fleeting achievement, is a genuine superpower in an unpredictable world.

The Body's Brilliant but Outdated Alarm System

Thousands of years ago, the stress response saved your life. If you were a hunter on the savannah and a hungry lion appeared in the distance, an almond-shaped structure in your brain called the *amygdala* would trigger a stress response, preparing your body to fight or flee by releasing hormones like cortisol and adrenaline, sharpening your focus, and increasing your chances of survival.[5] This response mechanism is innate, shaped by hundreds of thousands of years of evolution.

Today, the same system is active, but the predator today is no longer a wild animal. It instead comes in the form of back-to-back meetings, the never-ending emails, and the vague text messages that create a constant sense of overwhelm in everyday life. This happens because your brain cannot tell the difference between a hungry lion and your frustrated boss sitting in front of you. Both will trigger the same survival mechanism.

> **NOTE:** Stress is the default mind-body response to a perceived danger. Your brain is either signaling "danger" or "safety" at any moment.

Let's look at the physiology of this in more detail. In any given situation, even right now, your brain and body are constantly in communication, exchanging signals to assess your surroundings. A subtle, mostly silent analysis is always underway, scanning the environment for cues of safety or danger. Your system is continuously evaluating whether you are in a stable, secure situation or if there is a potential threat to respond to.

When you are in a familiar environment, surrounded by people you trust and feeling rested and present, your parasympathetic nervous system is likely active. In these moments, your brain signals to your body that you are safe. This activates your rest and digest system, which allows your body to relax, restore, and recover. If, however, you find yourself in a new environment, feel unsettled by a new project with unclear deliverables or are simply feeling down or exhausted, your sympathetic nervous system is likely activated instead. In this case, your brain tells your body that there's potential danger present. This is the system that prepares you to fight or flee, not from a lion, but from modern-day threats.

Do you know what your modern-day lion looks like? Modern-day lions that are likely to ignite a danger response in your body include meetings, emails, constant texts and notifications, lack of movement, processed foods, negative or limiting thoughts, shallow or restricted breathing, and an ineffective way of responding to stress. Modern life tends to send your nervous system more danger signals than ones of safety. This constant stream of perceived threats keeps your body in a low-level survival state, making it harder to relax, regenerate, and grow.

When stressful or overwhelming situations arise repeatedly, day after day and week after week, the brain begins to label them as difficult or unmanageable. This keeps your body, mind, and emotions in a constant state of activation, as if constantly preparing to fight the hungry lion. Over time, stress becomes chronic, even when no real problem or physical threat is present.

Critical Insight from the Classroom

During a workshop with a mixed group of corporate leaders, government professionals, and military personnel, we asked participants to map a typical weekday. One senior manager laughed and said, "So basically, I go from one fire alarm to the next until I fall into bed."

It got a knowing laugh—but it wasn't really a joke.

When we looked more closely at their days, a pattern emerged. The morning starts with emails before getting out of bed. Then traffic for those heading into the work space. Back-to-back meetings with unclear expectations. Notifications constantly interrupting focus. A working lunch. Difficult conversations squeezed between deadlines. Then the transition home—logistics, family needs, chores, more decisions, more emotional demands. Even evenings meant to be "downtime" are often spent half-scrolling, half-worrying about tomorrow.

From a nervous system perspective, this is a steady stream of **micro danger signals**.

Your brain is always scanning for cues of safety or danger. Not just physical danger, but interpersonal challenges, uncertainty, lack of control, time pressure, and unresolved tasks. Modern work and home life are filled with these cues. Constant connectivity means your system rarely gets a clear message that it's safe to fully power down. The result is not always dramatic stress—it's a low-grade, persistent activation that becomes your baseline.

(*continued*)

(continued)

Here's the critical insight: most participants initially try to solve this by wanting to "fix" the environment. Fewer meetings. Less email. A calmer boss. More help at home. And while some adjustments are possible, the collective realization in the room is usually this:

"For the most part. . . this is my life."

The pace of work may not slow down. Kids still need rides. Aging parents still need support. Missions, clients, and deadlines don't disappear because you're overwhelmed. This is where people can feel stuck—as if their well-being depends on conditions they can't fully control.

But the nervous system doesn't just respond to the environment. It responds to **your interpretation and regulation within it**.

Practices which increase a sense of agency, predictability, and internal regulation can shift how strongly the body activates—even when external demands stay high. This is the difference between being *at the mercy* of your environment and developing the skill of responding to it.

We saw this shift with one government participant who said, "I can't make my job less intense. But I can stop running it on redline all day." That meant building micro-pauses between meetings, using breathing to downshift his physiology, setting clearer mental boundaries when transitioning home, and recognizing early stress signals instead of overriding them.

The environment didn't magically calm down. But his internal state did.

That's the leverage point. When you strengthen your ability to regulate your nervous system, create moments of safety, and choose intentional responses, you stop adding extra fuel to an already demanding environment. Your Stressed Self may still get activated—that's human—but you recover faster and access your Best Self more often.

The Science of Stress and How It Affects Body, Mind, and Emotions

Stress affects each person differently. What one person finds stressful, another may not. What one person experiences as an unusual stress response may be a regular occurrence for someone else. Over the next few pages, we will explore the various ways stress impacts your thoughts, feelings, and behaviors (Figure 2.1), giving you a holistic understanding and a solid foundation for exploring your Stressed Self in Chapter 3.

You probably already know that stress is not always negative, right? Stress can be categorized as either positive (eustress) or negative (distress). Eustress occurs when we still feel in control of our lives, even when work, family, and other responsibilities feel a lot or even slightly overwhelming. This type of stress can be motivating, helping us stay productive and engaged. In fact, we all need a certain level of stress and activation. Without it, our mind and body go into standby mode. For example, remember a time that you had a job that was not challenging at all. If you are like our participants who had that experience

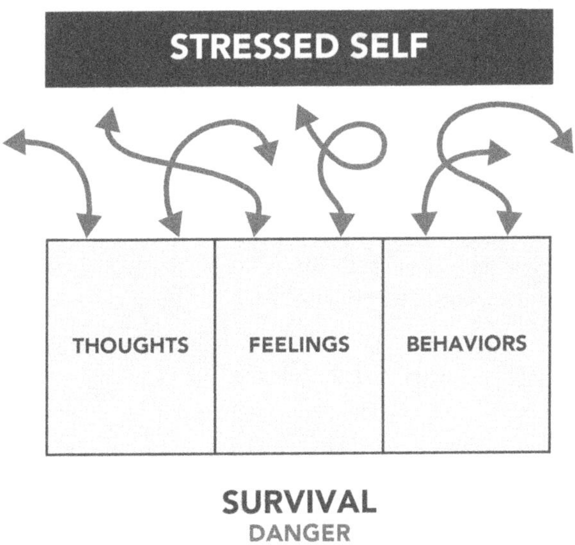

Figure 2.1 Your Stressed Self.

your energy was likely low, your focus was distracted, and your behaviors were probably not very productive.

However, the point where eustress ends and distress begins is different for everyone. It depends on mental, emotional, and physical stability, upbringing, and life experiences. Most importantly, it depends on individual perception. The way you interpret a situation plays a crucial role in whether you experience it as stressful or manageable. We will go much deeper into this point throughout the book.

Additionally, you may notice that you develop certain reactions and behaviors in response to stress. For example, you might distract yourself with Netflix or social media to avoid or numb feelings of overwhelm or anxiety. Or you may reach for coffee or other stimulants to stay focused and alert, without realizing that this can actually intensify your emotional response to stress. It is important to understand that these reactions are not the stressor itself. They are your way of coping with feeling overwhelmed, irritated, distracted, or tense.

To more effectively manage stress, you need to become more aware of your early stress warning signs, no matter how small they seem. If you only realize what is happening once you are already reacting and trying to soothe the symptoms, it becomes much more difficult to shift back to a more positive state.

Critical Insight from the Classroom

In one session, a participant summed up a pattern we see everywhere. He said, "Every night I run the video tape of my day in my head—what I said wrong, what I should've done differently, where I dropped the ball." Heads nodded across the room. Different roles, same habit.

Most of us carry around an invisible **retrospective scorecard**. At the end of the day, week, or month, we grade ourselves. How did that meeting go? Was I patient with my kids? Did I handle that email well? The intention is good—we want to improve. But the timing is off.

By the time you're doing the review, the moments are over. The conversations have happened. The tone was set. The reaction came out. You're trying to coach a version of yourself that is no longer in the game.

Reflection activates learning circuits in the brain, but under stress, your access to those circuits narrows. When you're in a stress response—time pressure, emotional charge, cognitive overload—your brain prioritizes speed and survival over nuance and reflection. So in the moment, you react. Later, when the system is calmer, your reflective brain comes back online and says, "*That's not how I wanted to show up*."

Cue guilt. Frustration. Self-criticism. Then the cycle repeats.

We saw this with a military leader who said, "I know exactly how I want to lead. I just don't do it when it's intense." A corporate manager added, "I'm a great parent in theory. At 8 p.m. after a long day? Different story."

The issue isn't that people don't know what "good" looks like. It's that their **nervous system state in the moment** is driving behavior more than their intentions.

That's why the shift is from retrospective performance management to **real-time response management**.

Instead of only asking, "How did I do?" at the end of the day, the question becomes, "What state am I in right now, and how do I want to respond in this moment?" That's where awareness, stress warning signs, and micro-recovery come in. When you notice the tight jaw, the rushed breathing, the urge to fire off the quick reply—that's the opening. That's the space Viktor Frankl described.

Small, in-the-moment interventions—a breath, a pause, a shift in attention, a quick reframe—can blunt the stress response enough to bring your "best self" capacities back online: empathy, perspective, impulse control, flexible thinking.

You may not win every moment. That's not realistic. But when you manage your state in real time, you start winning **more**

(*continued*)

(*continued*)

of them. One conversation handled better. One pause before reacting. One transition home that's more intentional.

And here's the payoff: when you do your end-of-day review, the story changes. Instead of a list of regrets, you begin to see evidence of alignment between who you want to be and how you actually showed up. The scorecard doesn't disappear—it just becomes a reflection of moments you actively shaped, not ones you wish you could redo.

When Helpful Becomes Harmful: Chronic Stress Explained

All of us experience stress, and not all of that stress is bad. In fact, as mentioned, short bursts of stress can help you focus, meet deadlines, or navigate challenging conversations. This is your body doing what it is designed to do and mobilizing energy to respond to a perceived demand. Maybe you've been in a situation before where you procrastinated on a task or project. Once you realized that you were almost out of time you were suddenly able to somehow mobilize all of your resources, mental, physical, even emotional, and pull a couple of all-nighters to perhaps even deliver great results. This can work for some people, on some occasions. Over time, however, this approach isn't ideal, as you are putting your system under immense stress.

What if the stress you are experiencing is constant and there is no time to rest and intentionally recover? For many people this is bearable for some time.

Critical Insight from the Classroom

In almost every group, someone eventually says a version of this:

> "Things are just crazy right now. Once this project ends. . . once the quarter closes. . . then I'll slow down."

There's always a future version of life where recovery will finally be allowed.

In one session, a senior leader laughed when he heard himself say it out loud. "I've been saying 'after this phase' for about 15 years," he admitted. The room went quiet—not because it was funny, but because it was familiar.

We tend to treat recovery like a reward we earn when the work is done. The problem is, in modern work and life, the work is never done. There is always another deadline, another issue, another demand. So recovery gets postponed to a fictional future that never quite arrives.

The problem, ironically, is that in the short term, this can look like high performance. Stress hormones like adrenaline and cortisol help you stay alert, focused, and driven. You feel productive. Needed. On top of things. From the outside—and often from the inside—it can look like you're thriving.

But physiologically, you're borrowing energy from systems that were designed for short bursts, not sustained output. The nervous system is meant to cycle: stress → recovery → stress → recovery. When recovery is consistently skipped, stress becomes the baseline. Sleep quality drops. Irritability increases. Focus gets compromised. Minor issues feel bigger. The body starts sending louder signals—fatigue, tension, headaches, digestive issues. Emotionally, patience shrinks. Mentally, creativity and big-picture thinking narrow.

We see this across sectors. The corporate leader who hasn't taken a real break in years. The military professional who can operate under pressure but struggles to switch off at home. The parent who collapses on the couch at night but never truly feels restored. Everyone is "pushing through," assuming that endurance equals strength.

But here's the critical insight: **recovery is not the opposite of performance. It is a core component of the sustainable human performance cycle.**

(*continued*)

(*continued*)

Our work consistently shows that sustained high performance depends on oscillation, not constant strain. Muscles grow in recovery after load. Cognitive performance improves when periods of focus are paired with deliberate rest. Emotional regulation strengthens when the nervous system regularly experiences safety, not just demand.

When recovery is absent, you may still get things done—for a while. But you do it at increasing cost. Over time, the Stressed Self shows up more often: reactive, depleted, less connected, less flexible.

The shift we see in the classroom is when someone says, "What if recovery isn't something I wait for, but something I build in?" That can mean micro-breaks between meetings, boundaries around transitions, real downtime without all the digital noise, or practices that actively calm the nervous system.

The future where things calm down on their own is unreliable. But the ability to insert recovery into the life you already have? That's within your gift. And that's what allows your Best Self to be sustainable, not just situational.

You may think that it will just be a few months until the project finishes, or that it's just a few more years until the kids have made it through school and activities. The problem is, most people do not know their personal tipping point. You may assume you know, but you don't really know what's going to push you over the edge. As things accumulate, stress becomes a part of your daily life—it becomes chronic. You have trouble falling asleep or sleeping through the night. Your mood has been low for weeks, you don't feel like engaging in your favorite hobbies, and you lack focus at work. On top of everything you feel rundown for no apparent reason. If you are reading this and thinking this is you, and that's just how it is, this is not the way it's supposed to be. And it's not the way it has to be.

Long-term or chronic stress really starts to chip away at your overall well-being, and before you know it you are in real trouble. And it doesn't need to be a serious illness or a job loss that brings you over the edge. It can be the small things. A missed meal. A couple of nights of poor sleep. A negative comment from your boss. A car that cut you off on your way home. You can ignore them. You can brush them off, but over time, when your system is already stretched thin, it becomes overloaded. These micro-stressors begin to stack up, and suddenly you feel disconnected from yourself, irritable, exhausted, and as if you're running on empty.

Stressors accumulate, and when the ship begins to tilt, it becomes almost impossible to keep it from sinking. Chronic stress is like expecting to successfully and safely navigate life while on a sinking ship. It's not going to work, and we've seen this happen again and again. You want to avoid your ship even beginning to tilt. And ideally, you want to protect it from even the smallest damage.

When people reach their tipping point, often more serious issues arise. Physical symptoms like digestive issues, persistent anxiety, muscle tension, or other illnesses begin to show up. People start to dread their mornings. They dread work. They stop doing the things they used to love.

Critical Insight from the Classroom

In one workshop, we asked participants to list the activities that make them feel most like their Best Self. The answers were consistent: time with close friends, being fully present with family, playing music, working out, getting outside, reading, faith practices, creative hobbies.

Then we asked a second question: "What's the first thing to go when work or life gets overwhelming?"

The room laughed—because the lists were almost identical.

When chronic stress ramps up we start unconsciously cutting ourselves off from the very things that regulate and restore us.

(continued)

(*continued*)

The corporate leader cancels dinner with friends because "this week is insane." The military professional skips the gym because there's "no margin." The parent drops the yoga class because it feels indulgent. The hobby that once brought joy starts to feel optional—even irresponsible—in the face of urgent demands.

From the outside, this seems logical. When time and energy feel scarce, you double down on productivity. You remove anything that doesn't look directly tied to output.

But physiologically and psychologically, this is exactly backwards.

Under chronic stress, your nervous system is spending more time in survival mode—heightened activation, narrowed focus, faster thinking, lower patience. In this state, the brain prioritizes efficiency and threat management. It becomes less motivated to seek out connection, novelty, or play—even though those are the experiences that stimulate the parasympathetic nervous system, release bonding hormones like oxytocin, and restore emotional balance.

In other words, stress changes your behavior in ways that remove your natural buffers against stress.

We've seen this clearly in participants who say things like, "I just don't feel like being around people," or "I don't have the energy to do the things I used to enjoy." It's not laziness. It's not a personality flaw. It's a nervous system that has been living in activation for too long.

The irony is painful. The very experiences that could move you toward Intentional Recovery—laughter with friends, a run outside, meaningful conversation, creative flow—are the ones that feel hardest to initiate when you need them most.

This is one of the clearest signs that someone is drifting from Best Self toward Stressed Self or even Forced Recovery. Social withdrawal increases. Play disappears. Life becomes narrower and more transactional.

> The shift begins with awareness. Instead of waiting to *feel* like reconnecting, you choose to act in alignment with what restores you. A short walk can change your state. A 30-minute coffee with a friend can recalibrate your mood. A yoga class can quiet a nervous system that words alone cannot.
>
> These activities are not luxuries. They are critical regulatory tools.
>
> When you are overloaded, your instinct may be to contract—to do less outside of work, to isolate, to grind harder. But what your Best Self really needs is connection and engagement in meaningful experiences.
>
> Protecting those anchors—relationships, movement, hobbies, quiet practices—is not selfish. It is strategic.

No one knows exactly where their tipping point is. Things just build and build. And then one day, your nervous system says, "That's it. No more. We're shutting down." You are burned out.

Some reports show that up to 75% of workers say they have experienced burnout. That's three in four people. And while it is absolutely possible to recover from burnout, it is a lot easier to recover while the ship is still intact.[6]

If you are wondering whether you may be in chronic stress mode, here are some signs that it might be time to make some changes:

- You wake up feeling tired, even after a full night of sleep.
- Your mind feels busy, anxious, or restless most of the time.
- You are less productive but working more.
- You feel emotionally drained, unmotivated, or disconnected.
- You are easily triggered or overwhelmed by things that never used to bother you.

If you are experiencing some or many of these signs, remember this is not just your personality. It's not normal to constantly wake up feeling exhausted. It's not normal to live in a state of anxiety or tension. These are signs that your body is asking for help.

Managing stress is not about creating a stress-free life. That is not realistic, and it is not necessary. The key is being aware of when you are stressed and having a plan to recover from it. Stress becomes a problem when there is not enough intentional recovery from it. Your nervous system needs time to reset. Your body needs space to rest and repair. Your mind needs moments of stillness and pause.

Even a minute or two of intentional rest can make a difference. This intentional rest might look like just closing your eyes and taking a few deep breaths while waiting in your car, laying on your back for a few minutes with your legs stretched up the wall. Or maybe taking your shoes off and standing barefooted in the grass or on sand. Or simply stretching your arms overhead, while laughing with a friend and just breathing. These aren't luxuries. These are your lifelines, tiny rituals that send a message to your body and brain that you are safe, that you are okay, and that you are allowed to slow down.

We will explore the concept of intentional recovery and provide specific strategies to experience it in more detail later. In the next chapter, we'll take the first step in establishing your foundation: becoming more familiar with your Stressed Self.

3

Recognizing Your Stressed Self in Action

This chapter is dedicated to you becoming very intimate with your Stressed Self. Part of you may feel a bit worried as you are reading these lines; maybe there's even some resistance arising. Maybe you are wondering why you should even become familiar with your Stressed Self. Wouldn't you rather avoid this version of yourself?

This is a fair point, and we invite you to stay open and curious as you move through this book, especially when doubt or resistance arises. Becoming familiar with your Stressed Self is essential for recognizing when you begin to act from that version of yourself. Without that awareness, you won't notice when you're reacting to stressors, and you won't be able to step in and respond effectively.[1]

So, becoming familiar or aware of something is absolutely necessary when it comes to creating new patterns of thinking and behaving. It is through those "aha moments" that you learn to shift from unconscious reaction to conscious response.[2] It's not rocket science, but it does require a willingness to look.

Reflection: Your Experience of Stress

Let's begin with a little reflection about the last time you felt stressed.

What was happening? Why were you stressed? (Example: "I had three deadlines and felt like I couldn't keep up.")

____

____

____

____

How did you react? (Example: "I snapped at my partner and procrastinated on the project.")

____

____

____

____

What were the consequences? (Example: "I felt guilty and more stressed afterward.")

____

____

____

____

Now, let's take this process a step further. Remember three additional experiences in which you felt very stressed and answer the same three questions for each additional stressful experience in the following space provided.

You are engaging in this reflective process for a few different experiences to increase your understanding and awareness of your patterns when you are experiencing stress. You must become familiar with your patterns to know when to employ the strategies we will discuss later in the book.

	Experience 1:	Experience 2:	Experience 3:
What was happening?			
How did you react?			
What were the consequences?			

Reflection: Identifying Your Stress Warning Signs

Now let's get a bit more specific about how stress shows up in your body, emotions, and mind. It is important to understand that your body is always talking to you in three ways:

Physically.

Emotionally.

Mentally.

The issue in our modern day is that we are so overstimulated and easily distracted that we have inadvertently trained ourselves to ignore the body's messages to us. What starts out as the body whispering to us via "feeling a little off," then gets a little louder by getting agitated a bit more frequently and feeling less energy, to eventually screaming at us in the form of overwhelm and racing thoughts.[3,4]

By becoming more familiar with your personal stress warning signs, you will put yourself into a better position to hear your body when it is whispering rather than ignoring it until it's screaming.

The intention of these practices is to create more awareness, not to fix or change anything. Even if you find yourself noting down what may feel like a lot of symptoms, rest assured, others are in the same boat.

Critical Insight from the Classroom

We were midway through an exercise on stress warning signs when a participant raised her hand. She said, "I just realized something. When I'm stressed. . . I hold my breath."

She went on to explain that during tense meetings or when her inbox spikes, she unconsciously tightens her jaw and stops breathing—not for a second or two, but for extended periods. She had never really connected it to stress before. It was just something she did.

Then she paused and laughed.

"I guess that's why my Apple Watch is always buzzing and telling me to breathe."

Now the room laughed with her.

For those unfamiliar, many smartwatches track subtle physiological markers and send a "breathe" notification when your heart rate variability suggests stress or sustained activation. Her body had been sending signals. Even her technology was reinforcing it.

So we asked what felt like a simple question:

> "That's great awareness. So what do you do when your watch tells you to breathe?"

Without missing a beat, she replied:

"I take it off and put it in my desk drawer. It's so annoying."

Cue even more laughter. That moment perfectly captures something we see over and over again.

It's not that people don't have stress signals. It's that they have gotten very good at ignoring them.

Breath-holding is a classic stress response. When the sympathetic nervous system activates—fight, flight, or freeze—breathing often becomes shallow, restricted, or paused altogether. This subtly reinforces the stress state. Oxygen flow changes. Carbon dioxide balance shifts. Muscle tension increases. Cognitive clarity decreases. You are literally depriving your brain of the very resource it needs to think clearly.

And yet, instead of responding to the signal, she removed the reminder.

Why? Because when you're in high-drive mode, interruption feels threatening. Slowing down feels inefficient. A device telling you to pause can feel like it's getting in the way of productivity.

However, that vibration wasn't the problem. It was feedback.

Your body is constantly communicating. Tight shoulders. Short breath. Racing thoughts. Irritability. Distraction. These aren't inconveniences. They're data. They're early indicators that your Stressed Self is stepping forward.

Ignoring them doesn't make them disappear. It just means the signal will get louder.

We often tell participants: don't treat stress warning signs as flaws to suppress. Treat them as dashboard lights. If the oil light in your car comes on, you don't put tape over it. You check the engine.

The goal is not to try to avoid stress—that's impossible. The goal is to notice it earlier and respond differently. Her watch wasn't being annoying. It was doing its job.

Take a moment to reflect on how stress shows up for you by answering the following questions. You can use the same situation you just reflected on or also think back to multiple situations to see if you find common stress signs. Don't overthink this and simply write everything down that comes to mind.

1. Physical Signs:	2. Emotional Signs:	3. Mental Signs:
Examples: "I get tension headaches," or "I wake up with a tight jaw."	Examples: "I feel frustrated," or "I feel tense."	Examples: "I start imagining worst-case-scenarios," or "I can't focus."

Critical Insight from the Classroom

During a workshop with a high-performing corporate team, we were mapping stress warning signs—physical, emotional, and mental. When we got to the mental category, the answers split the room.

One group said, "When I'm stressed, I lock in. I get tunnel vision. Don't talk to me. I just power through."

Another group said, "That's funny. When I'm stressed, I can't focus at all. I bounce between emails, Slack, my phone, back to the document, and I still get nothing done."

Same room. Same topic. Completely different experiences.

That's when we introduced an idea that tends to click immediately: **mental stress often shows up along a focus axis**.

On one end, you have **hyper-focus**. Vision narrows. You become intensely task-oriented. Peripheral awareness drops. You may miss context, tone, or relational cues because all cognitive energy is directed at the immediate demand. This is the brain in threat mode—prioritizing efficiency and problem-solving over reflection and connection.

On the other end, you have **hyper-distraction**. Focus fragments. You struggle to sustain attention. You jump between tabs, conversations, and tasks. You reread the same email three times. Your brain feels noisy and scattered. This, too, is a stress response. When the nervous system is overloaded, the prefrontal cortex—responsible for sustained attention and executive function—becomes less efficient. The result isn't sharp concentration; it's cognitive chaos.

Here's the critical insight: these are not opposite personality types. They are two expressions of the same underlying stress physiology.

And perhaps more importantly—you can move rapidly between them.

(*continued*)

(*continued*)

We've seen leaders go from tunnel-vision intensity in a morning meeting to restless distraction by mid-afternoon. A military participant once described it as, "I start the day locked in. By 1500 hours, I'm staring at my screen and clicking everything except what I need to do."

Neither extreme is your Best Self. Your Best Self operates with **flexible focus**. You can concentrate deeply when needed, but you can also zoom out. You can track the room. You can shift attention intentionally. There's cognitive agility rather than rigidity or chaos.

So the invitation is this: start noticing where you drift under stress. If you're hyper-focused, you may need a brief pause, a breath reset, or a quick check-in with the bigger picture. If you're hyper-distracted, you may need structure—one defined task, one timed block, one clear next step—paired with a short recovery moment to calm the nervous system.

Mental stress signs are not weaknesses. They're signals along a spectrum of focus. When you recognize the extremes, you can intervene sooner—and return to a state where your attention works for you, not against you.

Really contemplate on past situations and find those patterns of thinking and behaving that were early signs of stress. Some examples could be skipping meals, being short with or not listening to people, becoming very distracted, or experiencing poor sleep.

Recognizing your unique symptoms and early warning signs of stress is the first step in taking back control.

Action Step: Post Your Stress Warning Signs

As we said before, all of us respond to stressors differently, so it's important to identify and get to know your unique signs. Sooner or later noticing any of your warning signs will trigger a conscious reaction and awareness of a potentially stressful moment or stress response.

Since you are just beginning to recognize your reactions to stress and personal warning signs, it will be helpful to have visual cues that act as reminders. After training thousands of people on this process, the visual cues that we have learned are most effective are bright colored Post-Its that you place around your house and workplace. All that you need to include on these Post-Its are your stress warning signs.[5]

This seemingly simple awareness practice is extremely impactful for two reasons. First, at a basic level, your thoughts are made up of two things: words and images. You just wrote down words to describe your stress warning signs. Those words are not random. They came from experiences you have had in the past. Whether you were consciously aware of it or not, as you were writing down your words you were experiencing images in your mind about when you "were" those words. As a result of experiencing those specific words and images, you are already starting to become more familiar with your Stressed Self.

Second is a concept called *passive repetition*.[6] Think of your favorite song. Whether it's a current song or a song from years ago: it doesn't matter. When you first heard the song did you immediately rush home, print out the lyrics, and get the audio of the melody and then study both over and over until you knew the song? Not very likely. What likely happened was you heard the song and experienced it as catchy. Then maybe a day or so later you heard it again. Then maybe you searched it and listened to it. Then you heard it again a day or so later. And you continued to hear the song sometimes by choice and often in the background while you were doing something else. Then one day you hear the song and automatically begin singing along word for word with the melody as if you wrote the song. That is passive repetition. Your brain knows that something is important to you, so even when it is "playing" in the background, while you are focused on something else, your brain is taking it in over and over. . .without the need for you to actively choose to focus on it. This is what will occur when you place your Stress Warning Signs Post-Its in your environment. As you see these reminders on a daily basis, you will become more familiar with how your body, mind and emotions react to stress. . .without the need to directly focus your time and attention on the Post-It. This awareness will help you notice your experience of stress earlier and earlier, which will allow you to intervene sooner and decrease the likelihood of your stress response intensifying to the point of overwhelm.

Until your awareness of how your body responds physically, emotionally, and mentally to stress becomes second nature, keep the visual cues in place to help you stay connected to these signs. This will support you in recognizing them in real time and taking action when needed.

Where are the best places in your daily environment to post your Stressed Self words? Be specific and anticipate the moments and places where overwhelm and stress are most likely to occur (e.g., your workspace).

____

____

____

Understanding your Stress Warning Signs is the foundation that you will now build upon as you become much more strategic in your approach to more effectively managing your experience of stress. In the next chapter we'll use this awareness to help you move from reacting to responding to stress.

4

Your Gateway to Change

Many of our clients initially find it challenging to really zoom in on their Stressed Selves like we asked you to do in the previous chapter. It's almost like they do not want to experience that part of themselves. They tell themselves, "That's not really me," or "I do not like how I show up when I am stressed." And that makes sense. When we are operating from a stressed state, we do not feel like our best selves.

Critical Insight from the Classroom

In almost every program, someone says a version of this:

"I just try to keep it together."
"I don't want my team to see that I'm stressed."
"I put on a brave face and push through."

And to be clear, there are moments when emotional regulation is essential. Not every feeling needs to be expressed in full intensity. But there's a difference between regulating your emotions and **performing a completely different version of yourself.**

(*continued*)

(*continued*)

In one session, a senior leader admitted, "If I'm frustrated or overwhelmed, I double down on being upbeat. I don't want to bring the mood down." On the surface, that sounds positive. But then she added, "By the end of the day, I'm exhausted."

That exhaustion isn't accidental.

When you are acting in direct opposition to what you're actually feeling—smiling when you're depleted, projecting calm when you're internally agitated—you are engaging in what psychologists call *emotional labor*. This requires significant cognitive and physiological effort. You are running two systems at once: managing the stress internally while simultaneously managing the image externally.

That drains the human energy battery faster than almost anything else.

Your nervous system is already activated. On top of that, you're suppressing signals, monitoring your tone, filtering your facial expressions, rehearsing what you'll say so it doesn't reveal too much. It's like driving with one foot on the accelerator and one on the brake.

And here's the irony: while you believe you're protecting others from your internal state, most people can tell something is off.

Humans constantly scan tone, micro-expressions, pacing, and body language. When someone's words say, "I'm fine," but their physiology says otherwise, it creates ambiguity. The brain doesn't like ambiguity. Uncertainty can activate a subtle danger signal in others. They may not consciously know why, but they feel tension. They feel distance. They feel that you're not fully yourself.

We've seen this dynamic in teams where leaders think they're being strong by masking stress, while their teams privately describe them as "hard to read" or "not quite present." The dissonance creates subtle instability.

There's a powerful difference between "Everything's great!" when it's not, and "This is a demanding week. I'm feeling the pressure, but we'll navigate it together." The second response is vulnerable, grounded, and congruent. It aligns internal state with external expression. That alignment reduces internal strain and increases trust externally.

Appropriate vulnerability increases psychological safety and strengthens connection. When people see that you are aware of your emotional state and still steady, it signals authenticity and confidence—not weakness.

Your Best Self is not a mask. It's not the most polished version of you. It's the most aligned version of you.

When you stop spending energy pretending and start leading or living from a place of honest awareness, something shifts. Your battery lasts longer. Your relationships feel more real. And the people around you relax—because they're no longer trying to decode a version of you that doesn't quite match what they sense.

But here is the thing: getting to know this version of you is essential. Not to judge it, but to understand it and to meet it with curiosity, honesty, and compassion.[1,2] As Eckhart Tolle says, "*Awareness is the greatest agent for change*." And awareness begins with a willingness to look. You cannot change or adjust patterns and behaviors you are not aware of. If you are familiar with the stages of learning described by T. Earl Pardoe, you will know that when someone is still unconsciously incompetent, they do not even realize there is something they need to change. In fact, they are unaware that a problem exists at all.[3]

We both remember moments in our early work with clients when this became very clear. One of us heard a senior colleague describe someone by saying, "She doesn't know what she doesn't know." That sentence landed deeply. It expressed something we have seen again and again in our work. No real change can happen unless there is an "aha" moment, a spark of awareness, whether in someone else or within ourselves.

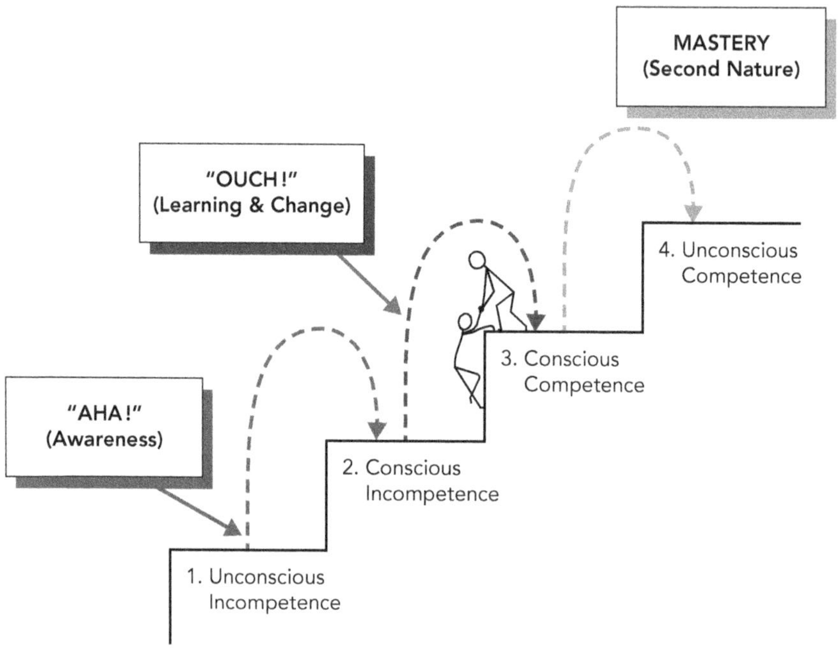

Figure 4.1 T. Earl Pardoe Stages of Learning.

Figure 4.1 explains the different stages of learning, from not knowing what you don't know to developing mastery.

After reading Chapters 2 and 3, we hope you now have a clearer sense of how stress shows up in your body, mind, and emotions, and how it quietly sneaks into everyday life. Often, it's not until you pause and say, "Wait a minute. I am waking up every morning and immediately grabbing my phone to check work emails. I feel anxious and agitated within the first five minutes after what was supposed to be a restful night of sleep. That anxiety carries into my day, turning into tension and leaving me emotionally on edge. By the time evening comes and I finally sit down to be with my family and enjoy time with my kids, I have no resources left. Instead of being present and joyful, I find myself irritated and frustrated with them."

The good news is that it does not have to be this way. If you are at the point where you're beginning to see the impact stress has on you, and you no longer want to accept it as a constant companion in your life, then congratulations. This is exactly where our real work begins, as we'll discuss in this chapter.

Activity: Experience Your Stressed Self

Now that you've explored how stress shows up in your life, we invite you to take a closer look at your Stressed Self by visualizing it. When you look at this part of yourself with honesty and curiosity, you begin to build the awareness needed to make meaningful change. The more clearly you can recognize and see this part of you, the easier it becomes to notice when it is present and choose a different response.[4,5]

For this activity, remember a time when you were your Stressed Self. Your task is to write a detailed and compassionate description of your Stressed Self by answering the following questions.

This reflection activity is extremely important because the more familiar you become with this part of yourself, the more power you gain to shift it when needed. As such, choose to focus your intention to complete this activity as one of understanding rather than judgment.

What do you look like?

____

____

How does your body feel?

____

____

How does this Stressed Self version of you speak, move, and interact with others?

____

____

How does being in the stressed state impact your work, decisions, and relationships?

____

____

Now take a moment to ask yourself:

What might shift in your life when you learn how to move out of this state more often?

____

____

____

____

What will it mean for your well-being and for those around you?

____

____

____

____

This reflection is not about judgment. It's about noticing. When you bring attention to these patterns, you create space for choice. You cannot change what you are not aware of. By becoming more familiar with your Stressed Self, you are already stepping into a more empowered relationship with yourself and with stress.

How to Shift from Reacting to Responding

Remember that most of us are not fully aware when we are stressed. We often don't notice until the water that has been boiling for some time starts to overflow out of the pot. By the time we realize something is wrong, we are already reacting on impulse. We fall back on old habits and conditioned responses without even noticing it. Maybe we haven't slept properly for four nights in a row but keep pushing, unaware of how stretched we really are. We instinctively reach for coffee after coffee. Or we gulp down lunch at our desks just to make it to the next meeting. We are on autopilot, moving through life in a learned response loop that brings short-term relief but no true resolution.[6]

Tired? Coffee. Angry? Yell. Anxious or restless? Scroll endlessly on social media.

Soon enough we have indirectly trained ourselves and our bodies that experiencing feelings of stress throughout our daily is "normal," and we forget what it feels like to be calm and relaxed.

It's human and it is understandable. But there is another way.

This is where the power of awareness comes in. As Viktor Frankl said, "Between stimulus and response there is a space. In that space is our power to choose our response. In our response lies our growth and our freedom."

So what does this shift actually look like?

Reacting is immediate and often emotional. It's what happens when someone sends you a passive aggressive message at work and you instantly feel your chest tighten and fire off a reply. It's your partner saying something triggering when you are tired and before you know it, you are raising your voice. These moments often come from the Stressed Self: feeling on edge, overwhelmed, and running on autopilot.

Responding feels very different. It creates space. It gives you a moment to notice the stress before it takes over. It may look like taking a breath before hitting send or choosing to walk away from your desk to get some fresh air before making a decision. It is the moment you feel the emotional charge rising and choosing to pause and think before speaking or acting.

Responding is not just slowing down. It's choosing. It's the ability to stay present and conscious enough to ask yourself, "What is truly needed here?" instead of falling into the same old loop. To respond means to meet a moment with intention rather than impulse. It is not passive. It's an empowered act of self-leadership.

Critical Insight from the Classroom

When we ask participants what gets in the way of being more intentional, more thoughtful, more responsive, the answer comes quickly:

"Time."
"I just don't have it."
"There's no space in my day."
"If I slow down, I'll fall behind."

It sounds logical. Most of the people we work with are operating inside tightly scheduled days—back-to-back meetings, constant notifications, competing demands at work and home. On the surface, slowing down feels like a luxury they can't afford.

But here's what we gently challenge in the room: **"I don't have time" is often a story, not a fact.**

Because what we're talking about isn't a 30-minute meditation session in the middle of the day. We're talking about 30–60 seconds. A pause before walking into a meeting. A breath before responding to an email. A moment to check in with your state before speaking.

From a nervous system perspective, even a short reset can shift you from stress response toward a more regulated, growth-based state. A few slow breaths can lower physiological activation. A quick mental reframe can widen perspective. That shift brings the prefrontal cortex—your decision-making, empathy, and strategic thinking center—more fully back online.

Now consider the alternative.

You rush from one meeting to the next without resetting. You're still carrying frustration from the last conversation. Your breathing is shallow. Your tone is slightly sharper than intended. You react quickly instead of listening fully. The meeting drifts. Tension rises. Clarification takes longer. Decisions are revisited.

What was scheduled for 30 minutes becomes 45.

We've seen this play out repeatedly. In one session, a participant reflected, "If a more thoughtful version of me walked into half my meetings, they'd probably end earlier."

That's the insight.

Let's say you take 60 seconds before a 45-minute meeting. You close your laptop. You breathe slowly. You ask yourself, "How do I ensure my Best Self is more present in this next meeting?" You notice any lingering stress and let it settle slightly.

That minute doesn't cost you time. See it as an investment in the next 45.

If you show up clearer, calmer, and more responsive, the conversation is more focused. You listen better. You ask sharper questions. You reduce unnecessary friction. The likelihood of higher-level output increases—and the meeting may end in 30 minutes instead of 45.

That 60-second reset just bought you 15 minutes.

More importantly, it improved the quality of the interaction and the experience for everyone involved.

When you're in survival mode, speed feels like safety. But sustainable high performance isn't about constant acceleration. It's about intelligent pacing.

Time is rarely the true barrier. The barrier is the discomfort of pausing in a system that glorifies urgency. Busy as a badge of honor.

Your Best Self doesn't need more hours in the day. It needs micro-moments of intentional reset within the hours you already have. And those seconds, used wisely, often give you more time back than they cost.

Imagine this: You're in a stressful situation. The reactive self might rush, lash out, or spiral into overthinking. The responding self pauses, notices what is happening, and makes a grounded choice. The external situation might not change, but your internal experience becomes completely different because you are not allowing the energy of stress to dominate and potentially gain additional charge as your day progresses.

This chapter has been your first step toward increasing your awareness. Without awareness, stress often hums quietly in the background, subtly influencing your decisions and behaviors without you even realizing. But the moment you begin to notice, something shifts. You step out of autopilot and into a place of choice.

The more familiar you become with your own stress signals and the way your Stressed Self tends to show up, the more space you create to respond rather than react. It will not always be perfect, but even the smallest shift in awareness can make a meaningful difference. Awareness becomes your anchor. Like the dashboard in your car, it helps you recognize early signs that something needs attention. It keeps you rooted in your values and connected to yourself, even when life feels overwhelming. And it gently reminds you that you always have a choice.

5

Meeting and Unlocking Your Best Self

Now that you have become more familiar with your Stressed Self, let's direct our focus on the version of you that you would prefer to be, your Best Self. It is time to get to know, explore, and unlock this part of yourself.

Now, you may not know this version of yourself very well yet, or maybe you even doubt its existence. Rest assured, this part can be found within each and every single one of us, including you. This part of you is real and accessible even though it may require a bit of time to connect with.

As you move through this chapter, you may find yourself being pulled back into your Stressed Self from time to time. This is normal, as meeting and unlocking your Best Self may be uncomfortable at times. If any warning signs of stress or overwhelm arise as you move through this part, pause and ask yourself: What about focusing on your Best Self is leading to feelings of stress or overwhelm?

Doing any work of self-development and growth will come with occasional growing pains. But for the most part this bit is likely to deeply inspire and motivate you.

Let's start with a couple questions to begin the process of getting more familiar with who you are at your Best.

What percentage of the time, at work and at home, are you currently showing up as your Best Self?

____

____

How did you determine your percentage?

____

____

If you are like us when we first got asked that pair of questions, our honest answer to the question, "How did you determine your percentage?" would be that it was a guess: 87%? 63%? 28%?

Why is your percentage likely a guess?

Because it is difficult to assess something you have likely never defined.[1]

So, let's get familiar with who you are at your Best, now.

Think of a time when you felt truly at ease with yourself, when things were simply flowing in all areas of life, and you felt engaged and in control of your emotions. What comes to mind? When did you last feel like you were your Best Self?

You may immediately be able to point to such a moment, or you may be struggling as the last time you felt this way was so long ago. Try to simply connect with that version of yourself without getting too carried away in stories and emotions. Notice not just how you felt within yourself, but also how genuinely connected you were to others.[2] A key sign of well-being is the presence of meaningful connection, while one of the first signs of stress is often "cutting off" genuine human connection.[3,4]

Devote a moment to describe whatever comes to mind.

____

____

____

____

____

Why Defining Your Best Self Matters

We will spend some time in this section defining your Best Self. For many, it is much easier to recall and connect to their Stressed Selves, so we need to clearly define how you think, feel, and behave when you are at your Best. Don't worry, if you have no idea and believe you have never met that part of yourself, you will soon.

When we ask participants to define this part of themselves in our programs, many answer "I don't know" or "I am not sure." This is understandable. After all, most of us were never taught to focus on and think about that version of ourselves that we want to bring to the world.

Critical Insight from the Classroom

When we ask participants to write down three words that describe them at their Best, something interesting happens.

The room gets quiet.

You would think this would be easy. These are accomplished professionals. Leaders. Operators. Parents. High performers. People who can articulate strategy, risk assessments, and five-year plans without hesitation.

And yet, when asked, "What are three words that describe you at your best?" we often hear:

"I don't know."
"This feels harder than it should."
"Can I think about it for a while?"

The discomfort is real.

In one workshop, a participant finally said what many were thinking: "I can tell you exactly what my boss needs from me. I can tell you what my team expects. I can tell you what my family needs. But I haven't really thought about who I am at my best in a long time."

(*continued*)

(*continued*)

That's the insight.

From the moment most of us wake up, our attention is directed outward. Emails. Messages. Children. Deadlines. Clients. Responsibilities. The brain shifts quickly into scanning mode: *What needs my attention? Who needs something from me? What problem do I need to solve?*

Over time, this outward focus becomes habitual. We become highly skilled at reading the room, anticipating demands, and responding to expectations. In many environments, that's rewarded. It makes you effective. Reliable. Valuable.

But there's a cost.

When your attention is consistently allocated to everyone and everything else, you slowly move yourself to the back of the line in terms of understanding what you need. And that's why, for many people we work with, being asked to define who you are at your Best feels unfamiliar—almost indulgent.

So if this exercise feels harder than it "should," that's not a sign that something is wrong with you. It's a sign of how practiced you've become at focusing outward.

The shift begins simply by noticing that.

One participant once said, after finally landing on her three words, "It feels strange. . . but also grounding." That's because when you define your Best Self words, you create an internal reference point. Instead of constantly calibrating to external expectations, you begin calibrating to who you want to be.

And here's the most important part: the fact that you're paying attention now matters more than how quickly the words come.

Awareness is the first move. Even the act of pausing to consider, *Who am I at my best?* begins to rebalance years of outward focus.

You are not selfish for reflecting on yourself. You are not self-indulgent for clarifying who you want to be. In fact, reconnecting with your Best Self is what enables you to show up more fully for everyone else.

Without a clear understanding of your Best Self, it's easy to become reactive, letting external circumstances dictate your actions. Over time, this creates a cycle where you're stuck in survival mode, unable to access the qualities that make you flourish.

This is why it's so important to define how this version of you thinks, acts, and feels and intentionally work toward embodying that version of yourself more often. Defining it will give you the clarity needed to know what you are striving for in all areas of life.

Exercise: Say "Hello" to Your Best Self

You will begin meeting your Best Self by answering a series of reflection questions. Take your time to really contemplate these questions and answer honestly. As you know, it is important to write your answers down for an even deeper connection.

Think about the characteristics you embody when you're at your best. Write down three words that describe you in these moments. For example:

- Playful
- Optimistic
- Engaged

What three words would you use to describe yourself at your best? Keep in mind that these aren't the words your family, friends, or colleagues might choose. These are your three words.

1. ______________________________

2. ______________________________

3. ______________________________

Remember that there are no specific words or characteristics that you "should" embody. Just answer honestly and authentically by sharing the first words that truly come to mind.

Once you've identified your three Best Self words, take a moment to reflect on how these qualities show up in your life.

When do you feel most aligned with these words?
Example: "When I'm collaborating with my team on a project I'm passionate about."

____

____

____

When do you struggle to embody them?
Example: "When I'm running late or dealing with a difficult client."

____

____

____

Action Step: Post Your Best Self Words

Now, similarly to your Stressed Self warning signs, where are the best places in your daily environment to post your Best Self words? Think of visible locations such as your desk, phone background, or bathroom mirror. Seeing these words throughout the day serves as a powerful reminder of who you want to be.[5] Decide now where you are going to post your Best Self words.

____

____

____

This simple action reinforces intentionality through passive repetition, a concept we described in the previous chapters on Stressed Self. We have experienced that participants who post their words often report increased self-awareness and a greater ability to redirect themselves back toward their Best Self during stressful moments.[6]

Now let's take this process a step further. Identify which one of your Best Self words gets compromised first during times of stress or low energy. For example, if one of your words is "patient," you might notice that impatience creeps in when you're tired or overwhelmed.

This word becomes your early warning signal that you are moving away from your Best Self and stress is taking over. By recognizing it, you gain the power to pause and make intentional choices before your Stressed Self takes the wheel.

So during experiences of frustration, overwhelm, annoyance, which of your Best Self words is the first to be compromised?

____

____

Your ability to operate as your Best Self isn't just about willpower. It's deeply influenced by your environment. Reflect on the following questions to better understand your environment and how it influences whether you feel at your best or stressed:

What environments and situations help you show up as your Best Self?
Example: "*When I have clear expectations and time to prepare*."

____

____

____

In what environments and/or situations do you feel that you fall short?
Example: "*When I'm dealing with ambiguity or interruptions*."

____

____

____

What is the difference between the two situations (when you are at your best vs. when you fall short)?

____

____

____

What small change can you make to create environments that support your Best Self?
Example: "*Start meetings by clarifying expectations*."

____

____

____

Many people underestimate the impact their environment has on them in terms of feeling their best or stressed. Creating more awareness here can help you develop strategies to show up as your Best Self, even in challenging situations. These small shifts can have a profound impact on how often you operate from that place.

Critical Insight from the Classroom

In one session, we ran what seems like a very simple exercise.

We asked participants to take out a sheet of paper and write down everything currently sitting on their desk.

Laptops. Multiple monitors. Two phones. Notebooks. Three half-finished to-do lists. Coffee mugs. Stacks of papers. Sticky notes. Chargers. Headphones. A stress ball. Snacks. A framed photo. A pile of unopened mail. More sticky notes.

Some people stopped at ten items. Others hit twenty. One participant laughed and said, "I'm at twenty-four, and I'm not even done."

Then we asked the question that shifts the energy in the room:

"What is your environment training you to do?"

That's when it lands.

Every object in your environment is a cue. So much of human behavior is not driven by willpower, but by context. We are highly responsive to environmental triggers. A phone on the desk cues checking. A visible inbox cues urgency. A stack of unfinished work cues pressure. Even a cluttered surface can subtly cue busyness and reactivity.

If your desk is filled with reminders of tasks, demands and incomplete loops, your nervous system receives a steady stream of "do more" signals. Without realizing it, you are being nudged toward the same patterns you've been running for years—rushing, multitasking, reacting, staying in high activation. Each item is reinforcing your typical behavior.

One participant once said, "My desk basically screams 'hurry up.'"

And here's the critical insight: **you cannot expect to create new behaviors in an environment perfectly designed to reinforce the old ones.**

If you've been operating in stress response—constant urgency, scattered focus, minimal recovery—and your workspace visually mirrors that state, it becomes incredibly difficult to shift into a calmer, more intentional way of working. The environment keeps pulling you back to baseline.

We often see this when someone says, "I want to be more focused," but their desk is covered in distractions. Or, "I want to take more recovery breaks," but there is no visual cue for breathing, movement or pause—only cues for output.

Change rarely sticks through motivation alone. It sticks when the environment supports it. That might mean clearing visual clutter. Removing nonessential items. Putting your phone out of reach. Adding one small cue that reinforces your Best Self—a card with your three words, a breathing reminder, a photo that grounds you, a notebook reserved for reflection rather than task lists.

These shifts seem small. But they alter the behavioral default as your environment is either reinforcing your Stressed Self or supporting your Best Self. If you want different behaviors, you need different cues.

One important point to note before we conclude this chapter: having the expectation that you should be at your Best all of the time is unrealistic and will only lead to an increase in stress.[7,8]

Here is the reason why you cannot be at your Best all of the time. In literally every situation, your brain requires two things:

1. **Certainty:** Knowing what is needed or what will happen next
2. **Conclusion:** Understanding how long something will last or when it will end

When either of these is missing, which they often are in our daily lives, your brain perceives the situation as a potential danger, making it harder for you to stay in your Best Self.[9] For example: A vague email from your boss might trigger uncertainty, pulling you into stress. An open-ended project with no deadline can leave you feeling unsettled and unfocused.

Vagueness or not knowing creates so-called "open loops." When your brain doesn't have certainty or conclusion, it keeps replaying the situation in an attempt to close the loop. This constant processing drains energy and creates stress.

Take a moment to think about the most buttoned up person you know. That person does not go to sleep every night with everything in his/her life certain and concluded. Neither will you. Instead, your focus needs to be on what you can do to become a bit more certain and how you can move a bit closer to conclusion with challenges in your life that are contributing to your experience of stress.

In the next chapter we will explain what typically happens when we experience situations where expectations are unclear (i.e., lack of certainty) and the duration of the experience is vague or unknown (i.e., lack of conclusion).

6

Barriers to Being Your Best Self

Now that you have become more familiar with who you are at your Best, in this chapter, you will gain a deeper understanding of how the constant demands, overstimulation, and distractions in your life make it difficult to be at your Best throughout your days.

Stress Responses and How to Shift Them

Every single one of us responds to stress differently. In fact, even our perception of what's stressful and what's manageable is highly unique.[1] Our past experiences and habits shape how we deal with stress.[2] Some of this is learned, some of it wired into us, but all of it can be worked with.

You may have heard the following quote from Viktor Frankl: "Between stimulus and response, there is a space. In that space is our power to choose our response. In our response lies our growth and our freedom."

Our response to any given situation is always ours to choose. This is an important mindset shift that people often need to make in order to allow change into their lives. You are not at the mercy of stress. You are not at the mercy of your bodily stress response. If you tell yourself, "*I can't handle this*," or "*This is too much*," chances are, it will be, and the physical, emotional, and mental reaction to the perceived stress will increase.

Responding vs. Reacting

Choosing to respond instead of unconsciously reacting requires an understanding of what's happening in a given situation at the level of your thoughts, feelings, and behaviors. As we discussed in Chapter 3 when we described the Human Energy System, all three influence one another. While we often find that our thinking influences our feelings, which in turn influence our behavior, it is not always a linear process.

Critical Insight from the Classroom

In one workshop, a participant shared that she hadn't been sleeping well for weeks. When we explored what was driving the stress, she said, "I'm pretty sure my boss is unhappy with me. I think I'm going to be taken off the project."

We asked gently, "Has your boss said that?"

"No."

"Has anything concrete happened?"

"Not exactly. . . it's just a feeling."

By the end of the conversation, it became clear that nothing definitive had occurred. There had been a shorter email than usual. A delayed reply. A meeting rescheduled. From those small data points, a full narrative had formed—one where her job security was threatened. And her body was reacting to that narrative as if it were already true.

This is something we see over and over again. Participants describe intense stress about events that haven't happened—and may never happen. A possible reorganization. A performance review months away. A conversation they're anticipating. A medical result not yet received. A future conflict imagined in vivid detail.

The nervous system does not distinguish well between an actual present threat and a vividly imagined one. If the story feels real, the physiological response becomes real. Cortisol rises. Muscles tense. Sleep suffers. Irritability increases. Focus narrows. In other words, we often enter our Stressed Selves because of a **story**—not a fact.

And here's the deeper layer: once the story takes hold, we begin reacting to it daily. We mentally rehearse worst-case scenarios. We interpret neutral events as confirmation. We behave defensively. We withdraw or overcompensate. The imagined future begins shaping present behavior. It's a powerful reminder that stress frequently starts with interpretation.

Our brains are prediction machines. They are constantly scanning for patterns and trying to anticipate danger. This is useful for survival—but in modern life, it often runs ahead of evidence.

One participant described it perfectly: "I'm reacting to a movie that hasn't even been filmed yet."

That's the insight.

When you notice yourself in stress response, it's worth asking: *What story am I telling myself right now?* Is it based on confirmed facts, or on possibility layered with assumption? This doesn't mean you ignore potential risks. Preparation is healthy. But there's a difference between strategic planning and living inside a narrative that hasn't occurred.

Your Best Self operates with curiosity rather than certainty. Instead of, "This is going to go badly," it asks, "What do I actually know? What don't I know? What's within my control right now?" Often, simply separating fact from story reduces the emotional charge.

We are meaning-making creatures. That's part of our strength. But when we forget that we are the authors of many of our internal narratives, we give those stories enormous power. Before reacting, pause. Check the script. Because sometimes, the stress you're carrying today is tied to a future that only exists in your imagination.

If you think, "I'm surely not going to get that promotion," your body may react with feelings of disappointment, sadness, or even resentment. As a result, you may actually start to put in less effort at work, avoid taking on more responsibility in new projects, or stop seeking active conversations with your boss about your professional development. From that lens, your possibilities for intervention in times of stress become very clear. In any given moment, whenever you find yourself in your Stressed rather than your Best Self, you can intervene in the following ways:

- Choose a different action (BEHAVIOR)
- Learn to regulate your emotions (FEELING)
- Change the story you are telling yourself about the situation (THOUGHTS)

In our programs, we use the word "reacting" to describe automatic and often unconscious actions that tend to pull you toward your Stressed Self. "Responding" means consciously choosing your thoughts, feelings, and behaviors in a way that brings you closer to your Best Self.[3] This is important because **any thought, feeling, or a behavior that you repeat during your day. . .you are training.**[4] It's like walking the same path in the forest every day. Over time, that path turns into a trail that becomes more and more established.

The more you repeat a reaction, the more automatic it becomes. Many people are unknowingly reinforcing their Stressed Self all day, every day. This keeps their mind and body stuck in a constant state of perceived danger, which over time damages your cells and drains your energy.

This is why it's essential to recognize both versions of yourself. The more clearly you can see when you are caught in stress and when you are living from your Best Self, the easier it becomes to shift.[5] The sooner you notice stress taking over, the sooner you can intervene and change course.[6]

Now that you are more familiar with both versions of yourself: Stressed Self and Best Self, your next step is to build greater awareness around your ability to assess your feelings in any given moment and if they are moving you more toward your Best Self or your Stressed Self.

7

Regulating Your Emotions

EMOTIONAL REGULATION IS a key skill that affects how you show up in your life. It influences your ability to be your Best Self. You have likely heard the term before, but now we will explore it in depth to build a clear understanding. This will help us all use the same language when talking about emotional regulation.

In this chapter as we focus on emotional regulation, we are zooming in on the feelings part of the Human Energy System. This is where emotions directly influence how you respond and whether you can access your Best Self or get stuck in your Stressed Self.[1] By understanding and managing your emotions or feelings, you can shift your energy from survival mode toward growth and safety, helping you show up as your best, more often (Figure 7.1).

To better understand a new concept (i.e., emotional regulation), it is helpful to develop a common language (words) and a model (images) that you can begin to apply to your own life. We're going to devote the next few pages to developing this intuitive model that you can use to self-assess your emotional state at any time during your day and then make an informed decision as to what choice you want to make that will move you closer to being your Best Self in the next moment.

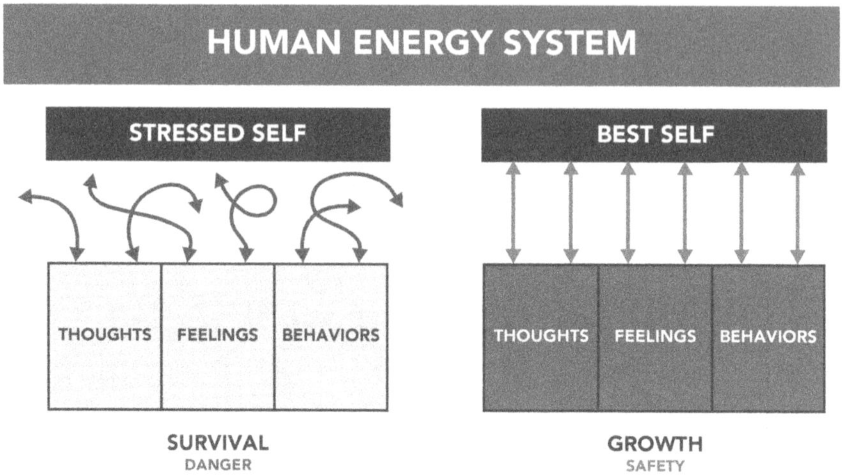

Figure 7.1 The human energy system.

A Model for Emotional Regulation

We are human beings who experience a wide range of emotional responses. Each emotion impacts us differently and influences our behavior. In our trainings we provide a model with two intersecting continuums of variables (Figure 7.2).[2] The vertical axis represents the quantity of your energy in any given moment, from low to high. Specifically, in any given moment is your brain telling your body that it needs to mobilize more energy or that it can conserve energy. The horizontal axis represents your physiology in any given moment, which can be growth-based, open to self-reflection, connection with others (safety signal) or survival-based, closed and guarded (danger signal). The intersection of these two continuums creates four quadrants of emotional energy. Each quadrant serves a purpose and benefits us in different ways.

To help you picture the horizontal axis, when talking about being open and growth-based, you can imagine spreading your arms wide as if giving a big hug. When in a survival-based state, imagine closing

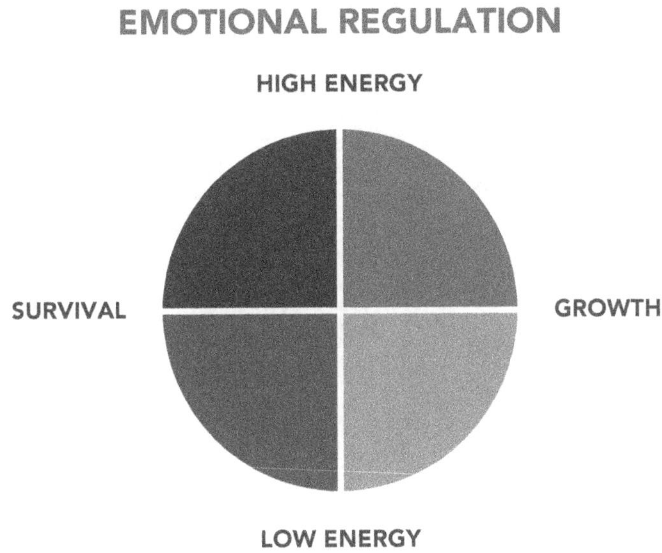

Figure 7.2 The four quadrants of emotional regulation.

your arms near your body as if protecting yourself. As we introduce each quadrant, we will remind ourselves whether it is growth-based or survival-based and whether the energy is high or low.

Now let's explore each quadrant and then discuss key insights across the entire model.

High Performance

We begin with the upper right quadrant (Figure 7.3). Here your physiology is open and growth-based while your energy is high. In this state you experience emotions that help you thrive by being connected to yourself and other human beings.[3]

You may find yourself in a flow state, building relationships and opening your mind to possibility and growth. Examples of emotions in this quadrant include optimism, hopefulness, focus, collaboration, challenge, adventure, empathy, and compassion.

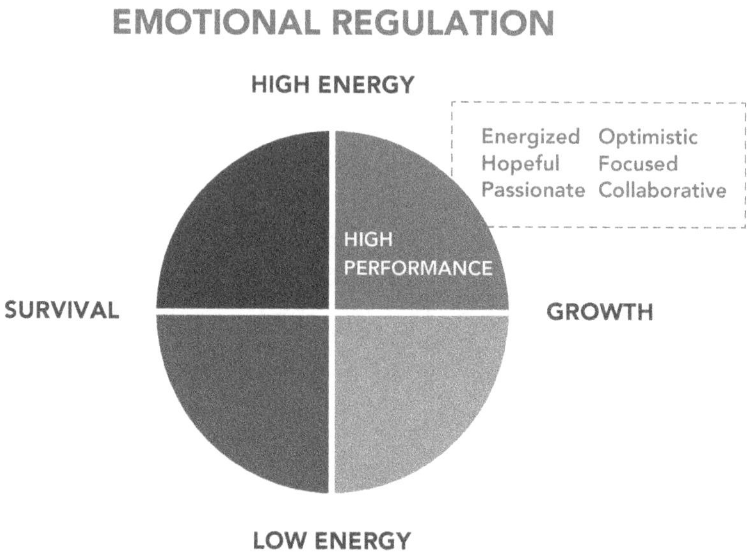

Figure 7.3 High performance.

If you look at your Best Self words you will likely see some reflected here. This quadrant is where high performance lives.

Write down two or three words that describe you when you are experiencing High Performance.

____

____

____

Then devote a moment to reflect on and answer the following question: What are some things you currently do at work or at home that help put you in a High Performance emotional state?

____

____

____

Stress Response

Next we move to the upper left quadrant (Figure 7.4). Here your physiology shifts to survival and closes, but your energy remains high.

In this quadrant you experience emotions signaling a fight, flight, or freeze response. Emotions such as frustration, anxiety, anger, defensiveness, and reactivity are common.

This state is critical for protecting you from danger or threats, but spending too much time here can negatively impact your health, energy, and relationships.[4] This is what we call the stress response. It is inevitable that during your day you will find yourself in this stress response. Remember, the stress response is your body's way of talking to or signaling you (i.e., stress warning signs) that your body is off track and you need to intervene.

Therefore, the challenge is not to figure out how to avoid the stress response, that is impossible, rather how quickly you recognize that you are experiencing it and then make a decision to do something to change your emotional state.

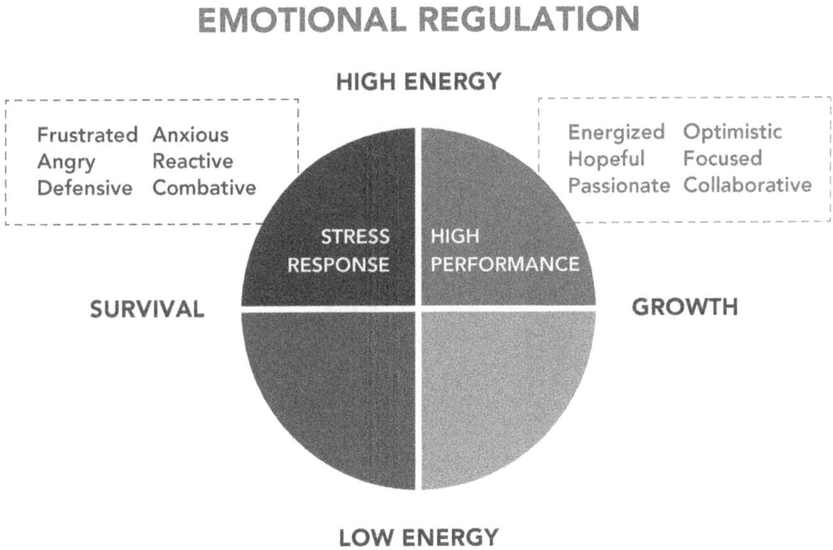

Figure 7.4 The stress response.

Critical Insight from the Classroom

In a recent session with a group of senior sales leaders from a global Investment Bank, a theme emerged quickly.

"When I'm under pressure, I'm at my best."

"I close deals when my back's against the wall."

"That edge—that intensity—that's when I perform."

There was pride in those statements. And rightly so.

In high-stakes environments like sales, the stress response can absolutely be an asset. When the nervous system shifts into high-energy activation, focus sharpens. Urgency increases. Tolerance for discomfort rises. You're willing to make the call, push the conversation, handle objections. That hard-edged drive can move things forward in a way that a completely relaxed state simply can't.

Let's be clear: the goal is not to eliminate the stress response.

It exists for a reason. In the right context, for the right duration, it fuels performance.

But here's what became clear as the conversation deepened: many of these leaders weren't just *using* the stress response strategically. They were *living* in it.

Deal after deal. Quarter after quarter. Pressure layered onto pressure. The edge that once felt energizing began to feel draining. Sleep was lighter. Patience thinner. Relationships at home more strained. Some admitted that when the quarter ended, instead of feeling proud, they felt empty or exhausted.

This is where the distinction matters.

The stress response is a high-energy survival state. It's metabolically expensive. The body cannot remain there indefinitely without cost. When you stay in that zone without intentional recovery, what begins as productive intensity gradually shifts toward chronic strain.

The insight we shared with the group was simple: **use the stress response, don't live in it.**

When you recognize that you've been in that high-energy push—negotiating, presenting, chasing targets—the next step isn't to keep accelerating. It's to shift gears.

Think of it like performance training. An athlete doesn't sprint continuously. They sprint, then recover. That recovery isn't weakness. It's what allows the next sprint to be powerful.

The same applies here. After a period of high-intensity output, you need to consciously transition toward intentional recovery. A walk between meetings. A breathing reset in the car. A clear boundary before walking into your home. A moment to decompress instead of jumping straight into the next demand.

And there's something even more powerful available in that shift.

The discomfort you just experienced—the pressure, the resistance, the stretch—contains growth potential. When you pause afterward, you can extract learning. What worked? What didn't? How did you show up? Where did you overextend?

Without that reflective recovery, you only get output. With it, you get development.

For high performers, this is often the reframe they need: you don't have to give up the edge. You just have to respect the cycle.

Stress response can help you win the deal. Recovery helps you sustain the career—and the life—around it.

Unfortunately, given the 24/7/365 demands and distractions that are chronic in our current lifestyle, many people unconsciously train themselves to function in this state to get work done. Remember, any thought, feeling or behavior that you repeated during your day, you are training. That means that if you are experiencing the majority of your day feeling anxious, frustrated, etc. that is the emotional state that you are training to be your default in all situations.

Write down two to three words that describe you when you are experiencing the Stress Response.

Think about how often you start your day in high performance but are pulled into the stress response by interruptions like emails, messages, or traffic. You may bounce back, but after one or two cycles you likely stay stuck in the stress response.

Devote a moment to reflect on and answer the following question:

What are some things you do at work or at home that often put you in the stress response emotional state?

The challenge with staying in this quadrant is that you are in survival mode, which closes you off from learning and connection and requires your body to remain in high energy. This issue is that the human body cannot be in high energy all of the time. If you continue to choose to push the body beyond its energy capacity each day, you will end up in the next quadrant.

Forced Recovery

Now let's look at the lower-left quadrant (Figure 7.5). Here your physiology remains survival based and closed but your energy level drops to low.

This is forced recovery. You may feel emotions like sadness, grief, defeat, and hopelessness. The key point to understand is that your body is going to get recovery (i.e., periods of lower energy) everyday, because it cannot remain in high energy all of the time. During forced

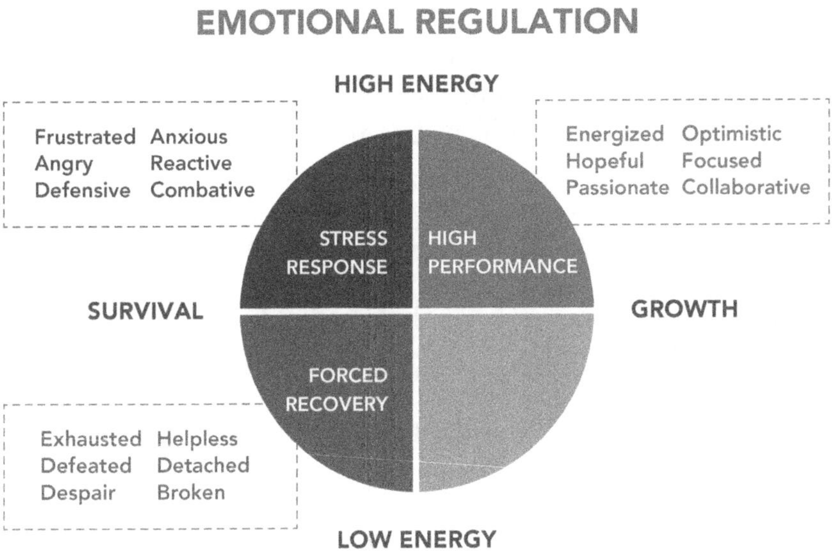

Figure 7.5 Forced recovery.

recovery, your body is literally forcing you to recover after you repeatedly chose to ignore its messages to you (Stress Response) that you needed to do something to get out of high energy.[4] In other words, forced recovery is your body making the choice for you to experience recovery.

A key sign that you are experiencing forced recovery is the experience of feeling detached from whatever it is you are doing and whoever it is you are doing it with. For example, when you find yourself going to social events or family functions out of obligation and lack any feeling of connecting to the people you are with and/or the things you are doing, you are likely experiencing forced recovery.

Write down two to three words that describe you in this emotional state.

____

____

____

Understand that everyone experiences forced recovery sometimes, but it becomes potentially harmful to your health and relationships if you start to experience it more frequently or daily. If forced recovery becomes chronic, after some time you are no longer experiencing forced recovery. You are experiencing burnout, which significantly increases the likelihood of you experiencing damage to your health, productivity, and relationships.

Critical Insight from the Classroom

In many of our programs, we ask a deceptively simple question: "Who or what gets the best and fullest version of your energy each day?"

The answers are almost always immediate.

"My job."

"My clients."

"My team."

"The mission."

There is nothing inherently wrong with that. Most of the people we work with are deeply committed professionals. They take pride in delivering. They want to perform well. They want to contribute. Giving strong energy to your work is not the issue.

The issue is what happens next.

When we follow up with, "And what's waiting for you at the end of the day?" the room shifts.

Family. A partner. Children. Aging parents. Friends. A hobby they care about. A community they belong to.

In almost every case, the people and experiences waiting at home are described as the most meaningful parts of life. The things that bring joy, connection, and purpose.

And yet, many participants admit that by the time they get there, their tank is nearly empty.

From a physiological standpoint, this makes sense. If you spend the majority of your day oscillating between high performance and stress response—both high-energy states—without intentional recovery, your nervous system is depleted by late afternoon. Cognitive resources are lower. Emotional bandwidth is thinner. Patience is reduced.

You may still physically be present at home. But internally, you are in forced recovery—low energy, withdrawn, less engaged.

One participant once said it this way: "My company gets the best of me. My family gets what's left."

That realization often lands heavily.

Because when you hit those important moments with an empty tank, the consequences compound quietly. You're quicker to snap. Less likely to listen fully. More prone to distraction. You skip the conversation. You cancel the activity. You go through the motions.

Over time, this doesn't just affect your mood. It affects relationships. Connection erodes not through dramatic conflict, but through repeated micro-moments of partial presence.

And here's the deeper tension: most people would say their family or close relationships matter more than their inbox. But their energy allocation tells a different story.

This isn't about working less or caring less about performance. It's about managing your energy intentionally so that the people and experiences that matter most aren't consistently receiving your lowest setting.

That might mean building micro-recovery into the workday so you don't arrive home depleted. It might mean creating a transition ritual between work and home—a short walk, a breathing reset in the driveway, a clear mental boundary that signals, *I'm shifting roles now.*

The goal isn't perfection. Some days will still be draining. But when you become aware of where your best energy is going, you can begin making small, strategic adjustments.

Because success at work is meaningful. But if it consistently costs you the quality of the moments waiting at home, the tradeoff becomes much heavier than most people realize.

What are some things you do at work or at home that help put you in the forced recovery emotional state?

____

____

____

Intentional Recovery

Finally, we arrive at the lower-right quadrant (Figure 7.6). Here your physiology is growth based and open, and you're operating at lower, more restorative, level of energy.

In this space you experience emotions such as calmness, peace, and relaxation.[5] Some of your Best Self words may also live here. This quadrant is intentional recovery.

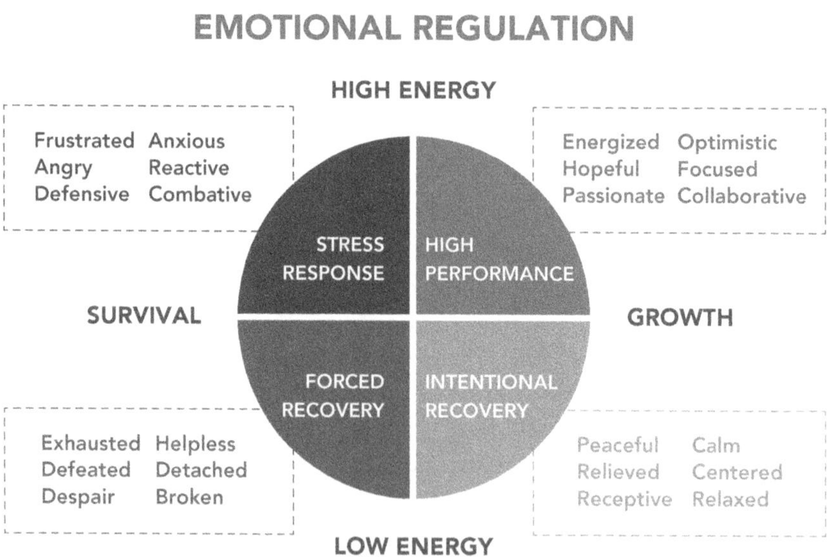

Figure 7.6 Intentional recovery.

Write down two or three words that describe you when you are experiencing this emotional state.

____

____

____

As we mentioned, your body is going to experience recovery each day. Forced recovery is your body choosing to get recovery because you chose to ignore its messages (stress warning signs) to recover. Intentional recovery is when you make a conscious choice to do something to experience recovery from stress, even if it is only for a few seconds. We define Intentional Recovery as a conscious, on purpose pause from "work."[6] The word work is in quotations because it can mean literal work or work from something like a long, energy draining conversation. Whatever experience you are involved in that is requiring your energy to consistently be used.

An important point here is that people often tell themselves that any moments of low energy at work mean that you are lazy, weak, or unproductive. The opposite is actually true; when these moments are intentional, they are vital to your ability to remain focused, sustain your performance and connection with yourself and other people.

Critical Insight from the Classroom

If there is one theme that shows up in every room—corporate, military, government—it's this:

> Recovery is something we'll get to later.
> "When this project finishes."
> "After the quarter."
> "When things settle down."
> "When I take a real vacation."

(*continued*)

(*continued*)

Recovery is framed as a future event. A reward. A luxury that belongs to a calmer season of life that somehow never quite arrives.

But there's another layer to this. Recovery isn't just postponed—it's often judged.

We hear powerful stories attached to it:

"It's lazy."
"It's indulgent."
"That's not how we operate."
"It sets the wrong example."
"If I slow down, the work won't get done."

These stories run deep. In high-performance cultures, constant motion is often equated with commitment. Intensity becomes a badge of honor. The person who is always on, always charging, always available—that's who gets praised.

But here's what many participants eventually recognize: those stories are just that—stories. And they are incredibly costly.

When recovery is consistently pushed into the future, and when slowing down is framed as weakness, people spend the majority of their time oscillating between high performance and stress response. Both are high-energy states. Both are metabolically expensive. Neither is sustainable without deliberate downshifting.

And here's the critical realization that often lands hardest:

Your Best Self is rarely fully accessible in constant acceleration.

When we explore the emotional regulation model in the classroom, many participants notice that their Best Self words—patient, thoughtful, creative, grounded, collaborative—tend to live in the intentional recovery quadrant. That growth-based, lower-energy state where you are present, open, and steady.

Not collapsed. Not disengaged. Just regulated.

Think about the hardest cognitive tasks you face during the day.

Finding the outlying data point that others miss.

Generating a genuinely new insight.

Listening deeply to someone who disagrees with you.

Influencing gently rather than overpowering.

Making a strategic decision with incomplete information.

Are those done best while hard charging at full speed?

Or when you deliberately slow down enough to widen your perspective?

Research on creativity, insight generation, and complex problem-solving consistently shows that the brain performs differently when it is not under maximal stress activation. When the nervous system is regulated and slightly downshifted, you gain access to broader associative thinking, empathy, and nuanced judgment.

In other words, some of your highest-level work requires intentional pacing—not perpetual intensity.

Recovery is not the opposite of performance. It is the gateway to your most refined performance.

The shift isn't to eliminate drive. It's to respect the cycle. To recognize that slowing down at the right moments is not indulgent—it is strategic.

When participants finally experience that their Best Self shows up most consistently when they are steady, present, and regulated, something changes. Recovery stops being a future event. It becomes part of how they work.

And that shift transforms not just their energy—but the quality of everything they produce.

What are some things you do at work or at home that help put you in the intentional recovery emotional state?

____

____

____

Putting It All Together

We covered a lot about each quadrant. The key things to remember are that you can experience different emotional states moment to moment. You will likely experience all four quadrants multiple times during the course of your day. By learning this model of emotional regulation, it will be easier for you to assess which quadrant that you are in at any given moment and then know what to do to move you closer to being your Best Self. Hint: your goal is to figure out how to experience moments of intentional recovery during your busy work day. . .even when you have little/no time. The good news is that you are going to do this in Part 2 of this book.

Awareness Is Key

Now that you have an understanding of emotional regulation, let's personalize it a bit more. Reflect on your day or week and identify moments that move you from high performance into the stress response. What kinds of situations cause this shift?

____

____

____

Increasing your awareness of these experiences is the first step to knowing when to incorporate a moment of intentional recovery, which will increase the likelihood of you showing up as your Best Self in the next moment.

The next step is to understand how you spend your emotional energy and help you take better care of yourself. Use the graphic below to reflect on how much time you typically spend in each emotional quadrant at work and at home (Figure 7.7).

Take a moment to fill in the percentages for each quadrant depending on how you have been spending the majority of your time. The percentages for work should add up to 100%, and the same goes

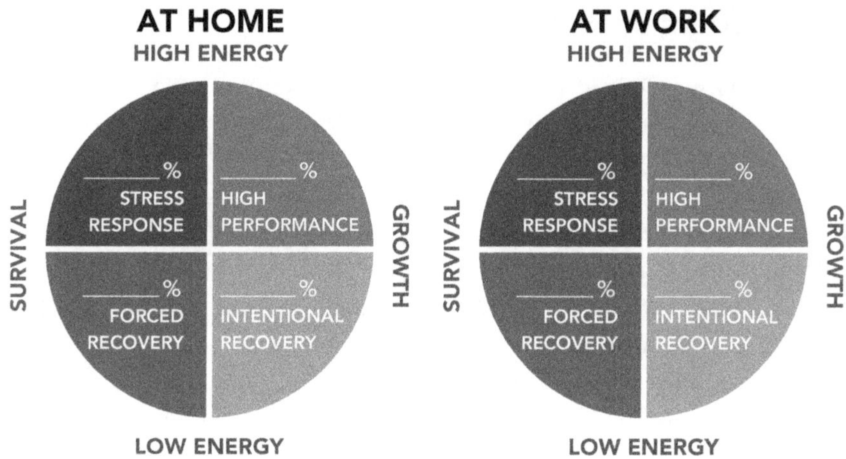

Figure 7.7 The percent of the time you have been in each quadrant: at home and at work.

for home. Think about the past six months as you complete this. There is no right or wrong answer here. Be honest with yourself.

Quadrant	Work %	Home %
Stress Response	_______	_______
High Performance	_______	_______
Forced Recovery	_______	_______
Intentional Recovery	_______	_______

What story are your responses telling to you?

____

____

____

Use this exercise as a way to increase your self-awareness and consider any adjustments you may want to make in how you manage your emotional energy between work and home.

The Concerning Pattern

Over time, a common pattern has emerged for many people. During the workday, most of us move between high performance and stress response, often without any meaningful recovery. This is extremely detrimental over time because both High Performance and the Stress Response require high energy. As we mentioned multiple times, the human body cannot remain in high energy all of the time.

As a result, when we get home, we tend to spend much of our time in forced or intentional recovery. The problem with this cycle is that exhaustion from work can leave us less present and engaged with the people and things we care about most. This fatigue can even spill into our weekends.

As we progressed through this section you have experienced thoughts like "I use home to recover," "I'm always in stress response," or "I find myself in forced recovery a lot."

This is why the focus on awareness is so important.

Becoming aware of your experience of stress is the single most powerful strategy you can develop. Without this awareness, no amount of tactics will truly make a difference. Later, we will explore how to build micro-recovery breaks into your day. Consistently incorporating these brief moments of recovery from stress will help you show up more fully at home and in life overall.

All Roads Lead to Intentional Recovery

Emotional regulation is about tuning in to the messages your emotions send you about your experience and your inner state. By reflecting on where your energy tends to go both at work and at home, you've taken an important step in understanding yourself better. There is much more we could write about emotional regulation, as entire books are filled with this subject. For the purpose of this book, we'll focus on cultivating awareness of the emotions experienced in each of these different states and how to use that awareness to know when you need to incorporate a moment of intentional recovery.

The key point to remember is regardless of whether you are experiencing High Performance, Stress Response, or Forced Recovery, your goal is to choose to do something that moves you into Intentional Recovery even if it's just for a few moments. And to do this consistently throughout your day.

Critical Insight from the Classroom

In one classroom, after walking through the full emotional regulation framework—High Performance, Stress Response, Forced Recovery and Intentional Recovery—we paused and asked the group what was standing out.

One participant leaned back in his chair, folded his arms and said, almost to himself, "I get it. . . all roads lead to recovery."

We smiled. "Tell us more."

What followed was one of the most concise and powerful summaries we've heard in any room.

"If you're currently crushing your goals in the High Performance zone, that's great," he said. "But you can't stay there without dipping into recovery to keep fueling it."

He was right. High Performance is a growth-based, high-energy state. It feels productive, focused, connected. But it's still energetically expensive. The brain and body cannot operate at high output indefinitely. Without intentional recovery, even your best days eventually degrade into fatigue or irritability. The system needs oscillation.

He continued.

"If you're mostly living in Stress Response—anxious, reactive, frustrated—it's very hard to get back to High Performance without at least a momentary reset in recovery."

Again, exactly right. When you're in Stress Response, your physiology is in survival mode. Focus narrows. Flexibility decreases. Empathy and creativity drop. Trying to force your way directly from stress into peak performance rarely works. The nervous system needs a downshift first. Even a brief recovery moment—a breath reset, a walk, a pause—can calm activation enough to bring your higher-level thinking back online.

(continued)

(*continued*)

Then he finished with this:

> "And if you're predominantly in Forced Recovery—low energy, detached, flat—you have to get intentional, or you'll slide into burnout."

Forced Recovery is what happens when the body takes recovery into its own hands. Energy drops. Engagement fades. You may feel numb or disconnected. If you don't intentionally intervene—through restorative behaviors, boundaries, reflection, and support—that state can deepen into chronic depletion.

What struck the room was how elegant the pattern was.

No matter where you start—High Performance, Stress Response, or Forced Recovery—the sustainable path forward runs through Intentional Recovery.

Recovery isn't a detour. It's the junction point.

It fuels High Performance.

It resets Stress Response.

It prevents Forced Recovery from becoming burnout.

Many participants come into the training thinking recovery is optional—something nice to have if time allows. But when they see the model as a dynamic system rather than isolated quadrants, the logic becomes undeniable.

You can sprint. You can push. You can grind. But eventually, the body will collect its due.

The most effective performers aren't the ones who avoid stress or live in permanent calm. They're the ones who understand the cycle—and respect it.

"All roads lead to recovery" wasn't just a clever summary.

It was a recognition that if you want sustainable access to your Best Self, recovery isn't the reward at the end.

It's the mechanism that makes everything else possible.

We're going to describe the practice of Intentional Recovery in much more detail in the next chapter.

8

Defining Intentional Recovery

WHAT IF THE key to becoming more focused, grounded, emotionally available, and sustainably productive wasn't about doing more, but learning how to pause with purpose?

Most high-performing individuals believe that rest is something they earn. Recovery is often scheduled only after the deadlines, after the meetings, after the launch, or after the kids are asleep, if it's scheduled at all. But what if you could begin to recover while you work, while you parent, and while you build your life?

In this chapter, we'll explore the practice of intentional recovery. It's not about long weekends or waiting for a perfect vacation. It's about weaving small, deliberate moments of rest into your daily rhythm so you stop crashing and start living with more clarity and presence.

What Is Intentional Recovery?

Intentional recovery is a conscious decision to pause and recharge your energy. You are purposefully choosing to pause form work. That work can be literal work, a lengthy conversation, disagreement, event, etc. Any experience that is requiring your energy for an extended period of time.

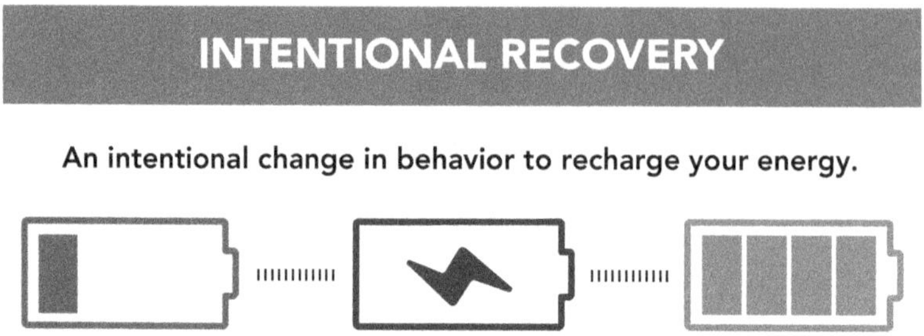

Figure 8.1 Your human energy battery.

Intentional recovery is not passive, and it's certainly not a luxury. It is a strategic way to regulate your emotions, reset your mental state, and shift how you show up in your day.[1] When you begin to treat recovery as a part of your workflow rather than a reward for finishing it, you create more stability, capacity, and emotional range.

Our bodies and minds need recovery the same way our phones need to be recharged.[2] The difference is, your phone has a battery indicator. You can see when it hits 15% or when it flashes red at 3%. But most of us don't notice our own internal warning signs until we've already hit a wall.

That's where intentional recovery comes in. It helps you build awareness around when your energy is dipping and gives you tools to restore it before your human battery runs out of charge (Figure 8.1).

The 1% Rule

One of the most common misconceptions about recovery is the belief that a break should bring you all the way back to 100% charge on your human energy battery. You step outside for five minutes, expect to feel refreshed, and then get frustrated when you're still tired. But this expectation is not only unrealistic, it keeps people from choosing to intentionally recover at all.

The real goal of intentional recovery is to gain back just 1% or 2% of battery charge at a time over the course of your day.[3] One percent here, another there, another later, etc. Such that if you're ending your day at 3% battery life and showing up at home totally depleted, the aim isn't to come home fully recharged. It's to arrive with 10%–12% charge remaining on your human energy battery. That difference may seem negligible, but it fundamentally changes how you respond to your family, your partner, your body, and your own inner world.

By stacking these tiny moments of intentional recovery throughout your day, you are creating space for your human energy system to recalibrate back into the safety signal bringing more energy back into your system.

Why We Don't Prioritize Recovery

Even when we understand how important it is, most of us don't build recovery into our days. It often gets pushed aside because you tell yourself that it is unproductive.[4] In some environments, it's even directly or indirectly perceived as a weakness. As a result, you might tell yourself that you don't have time, or that once everything is done you will choose to experience some recovery.

But recovery doesn't require a day off or hours of free time. It can be as simple as a one-minute breath reset, a five-minute walk, or a fifteen-minute break to sit in silence, close your eyes, or drink a cup of tea without distraction.[5] These small choices accumulate. They change how you feel, how you think, and how you relate to yourself and others.

Recognizing the Signs

The more you begin to pay attention, the more you'll notice your body's own battery indicators (i.e., your Stress Warning Signs). Maybe you're short-tempered, unable to focus, or feeling foggy. Maybe your joints feel stiff or you find yourself scrolling for longer than you intended. These are all signals that your human energy battery is draining and needs a recharge. Once you recognize these signs, you can take action, not to fix everything, but to add 1 or 2% back into your system. We will go into much more detail about how to do this when we discuss strategies in Part 2 of the book.

Coming back to the phone battery analogy, when it's down to 10%, you probably start scanning for chargers. You may even change your behavior, lower the screen brightness, close apps, or stop streaming. But most of us don't extend that same care or awareness to ourselves. We expect to function with emotional clarity, patience, and creativity at 3% without ever plugging in. That's what intentional recovery helps you change. You begin to notice when you're low and gently plug yourself back into a source, whatever that may be for you.

A Note on Effort

Let's be real. If you're coming home every evening fully charged and relaxed, you're probably not doing much during the day. It's called work for a reason. This chapter isn't about eliminating effort or stress. It's about making sure that your output is balanced with moments of restoration so you don't lose access to your Best Self in the process.

In the next section, we'll map out how energy flows through your day. Where it's going out, where it's coming in, and how you can start to create more of what you actually need to sustain your life and not just survive it.

Plotting Your Current Recovery

Now that you have a sense of the general stress and recovery rhythm throughout your day, take a moment to plot your own pattern (Figure 8.2). You will notice that the horizontal axis ranges from 6 a.m.

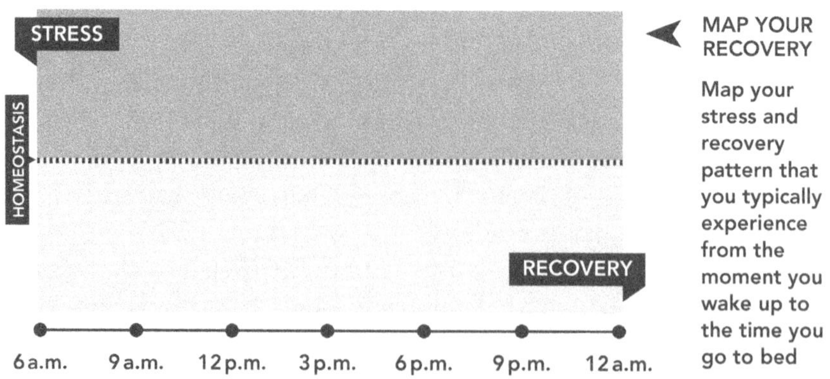

Figure 8.2 Plotting your stress and recovery pattern.

to midnight. Feel free to adjust it to reflect your typical day from the moment your eyes open to the time you go to sleep.

Start by thinking through your usual routine. Where in your day are you mobilizing a lot of energy (i.e., Energy Out), dealing with pressure or focusing on demanding tasks? Mark those moments higher on the graph to show energy going out. Then consider the moments where you feel yourself settling, exhaling, or actively bringing energy back into your system (i.e., Energy In). These are your recovery times, and they can be just as significant. The more deeply you recover in a given moment, the higher that point should be placed on the recovery side of the diagram. This is not about perfection. There is no right answer. Simply map the flow of your energy in and out as you normally experience it.

Once you finish, take a look at the shape of your stress & recovery pattern. What is it revealing to you? Perhaps you notice long stretches without recovery. Or maybe you already have a good rhythm between energy out and energy in. Either way, see if you can identify what helps you stay balanced in those moments and ask yourself whether any of those habits or strategies could be used more intentionally in other parts of your day.

One note: exercise can land on either side. It might feel intense and activating, or it might feel like release and regulation. Choose based on how it lands in your own body. Let your diagram tell the real story of your energy rhythm without judgment and then let it guide you toward what might need to shift.

Critical Insight from the Classroom

One of the most overlooked concepts in our stress and recovery oscillation framework is the dotted line that runs through the middle of the model.

We call it the **line of homeostasis**.

When you are on that line, you are not actively in stress response. Your heart rate isn't elevated. Your thoughts aren't

(*continued*)

(*continued*)

racing. You're not pushing hard. But you're also not intentionally recovering. You're neutral. Baseline. Coasting.

And this is where a lot of low-hanging fruit slips through people's fingers.

There is a common assumption that when a stressful moment ends, recovery naturally begins.

It doesn't.

The end of stress simply means the stressor has passed. It does not automatically move your nervous system into restoration mode. It just returns you to homeostasis—not stressed, but not replenished either.

In one session, a participant was mapping her day across the quadrants. She described her early morning run as stress—physical energy expenditure, elevated heart rate, pushing her limits.

We nodded. "Great. So how do you recover from your run?"

She paused. "I stop running."

The room laughed. She laughed too.

And we said, "Stopping running means you're no longer adding stress. But does it mean you've recovered?"

That's when it clicked.

If you finish a hard run and immediately jump into emails, skip hydration, don't stretch, and refuel poorly, you may not be actively stressing the body anymore—but you're not actively recovering either.

We asked her, "What would intentional recovery from that run actually look like?"

"Stretching," she said. "Drinking water. Getting some calories back into the system."

"Bingo," we said. "That's recovery."

Those actions move you **below the line of homeostasis**—into the intentional recovery zone where growth actually happens.

The same principle applies to your workday.

You finish a tense meeting. The meeting ends. Stress over.

But do you immediately open your inbox? Jump into the next call? Scroll your phone?

If so, you've returned to homeostasis at best—and often straight back into activation. You haven't leveraged the previous stress for growth.

In physiology, adaptation happens during recovery. Muscles rebuild after load. Insight consolidates after cognitive effort. Emotional resilience strengthens when activation is followed by restoration.

If you want to use stress as a growth tool rather than a depletion cycle, you must actively step into recovery.

That might mean a two-minute breathing reset after a difficult conversation. A short walk after a high-stakes presentation. Hydrating. Stretching. Pausing. Reflecting briefly on what you learned.

The distinction is subtle but powerful:

Not experiencing stress is not the same as recovering.

Homeostasis is neutral. Recovery is intentional.

And when you begin recognizing the small transitions throughout your day—the end of a meeting, the completion of a task, the close of a call—you'll see opportunities everywhere to move below that dotted line, even briefly.

Those are the moments where resilience is built.

Not by avoiding stress.

But by deliberately recovering from it.

Oscillation

A typical high-performing day is not one without stress. It's one where you are able to move between effort and renewal with intention. This natural rhythm is called *oscillation*. Oscillation is the strategic balance between energy going out of your Human Energy System and energy

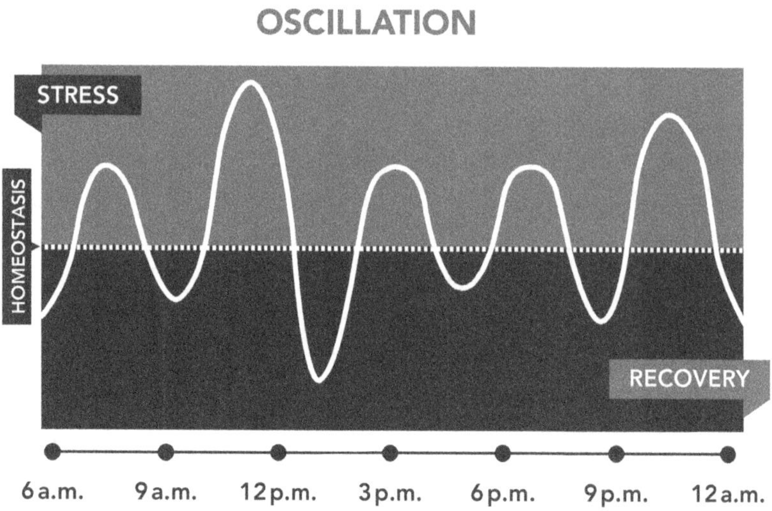

Figure 8.3 Ideal oscillation pattern: stress followed by recovery.

coming into your Human Energy System (Figure 8.3). "Energy out" happens when you are performing, focused, mobilized, or navigating demands. "Energy In" happens when you take time to restore, reset and bring yourself back to a more balanced state.

Stress itself is not the problem. It becomes a problem when it is not followed by recovery. If your day includes far more output than renewal, you may feel stretched thin, reactive, or depleted. If your day includes too much downtime without challenge, you may feel disengaged or under-stimulated. Neither end of the spectrum supports your full capacity. The goal is not to have a perfect balance at every moment, but rather to pay attention to how you oscillate throughout the day and make intentional choices about when and how to recover. The quality of those moments matters more than their length. A five-minute pause, a short walk, or even a few breaths can help reset your system.

The key is to seek out those moments of renewal before stress accumulates. The sooner you can bring energy back in after a demanding moment, the more sustainably you can remain connected to yourself and show up for what matters most to you.

The Foundation Is Set

At this point you have set your foundation by gaining greater awareness of the following:

- The difference between stress and stressors
- Your personal stress warning signs
- Who you are at your Best
- Emotional regulation
- The importance of Intentional Recovery

In Part 2 we will share specific, science-based strategies to both decrease the level of stress you experience in your mind and body and increase the moments of intentional recovery you take during the course of your day.

PART II

Strategies

"We are what we repeatedly do. Excellence, then, is not an act but a habit."

—Aristotle

9

A New Way Forward

For years in the productivity and self-management literature, the recommendation has been to shift from managing your time to managing your energy.[1] Time is fixed. We all get 24 hours in a day. But energy, when managed wisely, can be renewed and sustained.

The challenge for most people is how.

Knowing how to structure your day based on your personal recovery needs and aligning that with your daily tasks is one of the most important skills you can learn.[2] If you are not actively managing your energy, especially your intentional recovery, then you are effectively giving control of your energy to someone else. And that someone is not going to prioritize your needs over theirs.

Intentional recovery, breaks, and rest are not luxury items for when things calm down. They are essential to thriving.[3] Still, most people focus narrowly on making better use of their limited energy rather than learning how to expand their total capacity for it.

On top of that, since most of us never received real training on how to respond to stress in healthier or more productive ways, we often end up reinforcing the stress reaction. Instead of learning how to create a life that isn't filled with perceived threats (i.e., danger signal) and pressure around every corner, we simply become more effective at handling the pressure and intentionally experiencing moments in the safety signal.[4]

Life does not need to be designed around constant stress and high alert.[5] Understanding this new perspective is often an eye-opener for our program participants, changing the way they see themselves and the world around them.

In this part of the book, we will focus on changing feelings and thoughts, as these are the two other key aspects of the human energy system that will help you be and feel at your best. Behaviors are simplest to implement and change, so it makes sense we started there. Yet the feelings and thoughts under the surface strongly influence us on all levels. They are usually more difficult to change. But it's not impossible.

Feelings or emotions, as you may have experienced, strongly drive your behaviors at any moment.[6] For example, if you are feeling tired or low on energy, you may skip getting movement or exercise that day.[7] Thoughts are the basis of all our feelings and actions, but they are much harder to access. This is why we will end the section with reflections on the concept of storytelling (i.e., your inner narrative). Once we learn how to effectively access, challenge, and change our thinking, we unlock a true superpower and a direct path to our Best Self.

In this part we will share the "how" to be more intentional about managing your experience of stress more effectively. At IHP, we believe in sharing techniques and tools that, when implemented consistently, provide you with the quickest and most promising return to your Best Self. For us, it is important that the strategies are simple, practical, can be used anywhere and at any time without the need for any gadgets or external resources, and most importantly, they are things that you will actually do.

Impactful Behaviors for Recovery

Throughout the next chapters, we'll explore very specific behaviors related to movement, hydration, breathing, and sleep that are proven to support being at your best. While there are many potential behavioral suggestions we could share, we'll focus on the ones that meet the following criteria:

- They provide non-linear returns, meaning that for every "one unit of energy" you put into these behaviors, you'll experience two to three times the "return" in recovery, focus, and energy.
- They do not require any additional resources (technology, wearables, etc.).
- They can be done anywhere at any time.

These strategies are designed not only to help you rest and recover but also to prevent burnout in the future. When practiced consistently, they will help you approach life's challenges with more ease, clarity, and confidence.

Movement, hydration, breathing, and sleep are fundamental to your overall health, which is exactly why they matter so much during intense or stressful times.[8,9,10] Yet often, as stress and overwhelm increase, these very behaviors are the first to be neglected. This can create a vicious cycle that actually increases your experience of stress.

You may wonder why we are not starting with thoughts and feelings. Thoughts can be persistent, often unconscious, and are not easy to shift quickly.[11] They can change, but it usually takes time and attention. Feelings are also largely automatic and require practice to work with skillfully. In the heat of the moment when you're feeling stressed, your thoughts and feelings are often harder to access because your brain shifts into "danger" mode, triggering unconscious reactions. In contrast, observing and shifting your behavior is often the most direct and accessible way to bring some relief, especially in the heat of a stressful moment.[12]

That is why we will begin here. These intentional recovery behaviors are not designed to remove stress, but they do expand your capacity to respond to it much more effectively. Each one of these offers a practical way to return to center and move forward with presence, steadiness, and strength.

Let's begin in the following chapter with movement.

10

Moving to Thrive

In modern life, many of us spend most of our waking hours sitting. We sit at desks, in cars, at the dinner table, and in front of screens. While this may feel normal, the body is not designed for such long periods of stillness. Prolonged sitting has profound effects on both physical health and mental well-being.

Dr. James Levine, a professor at the Mayo Clinic, famously coined the phrase "*sitting is the new smoking*." That is because extended sitting has been linked to an increased risk of cardiovascular disease, metabolic syndrome, type 2 diabetes, certain cancers, and early death.[1] Even mental health can be affected, with inactivity contributing to symptoms of depression and anxiety.[2]

In our work we have found that the stress-related issues are not just the result of sitting for most of the day, but in the broader trap of prolonged sedentariness, which includes both extended sitting and nearly immobile standing. The combination of the two amplifies stress on your mind and body, which almost always results in a cascade of long-term health issues.[3] If you're like most of our training participants, your body remains basically still for hours (typing and talking on your phone do not count as movement), hunched over a screen or standing upright without shifting. This lack of movement actually causes your body more stress because as you read your texts and emails, sit in your meetings, work on your projects you are constantly telling your body to generate more energy (i.e., be in High Energy). The body's natural way to keep that energy flowing is through movement. By continuing to signal the body to be in High Energy while at the same time, limiting its movement (i.e., its flow of that energy) you are causing your body to experience more stress.

Engaging in these detrimental sedentary practices over time ultimately results in increased vulnerability to experiencing anxiety, depression, and chronic fatigue as well as joint compression (pain), muscle atrophy, and impaired circulation. The point is that our bodies are designed to move consistently and the chronic lack of movement that defines our current lifestyle undermines the body's natural defenses against inflammation, hormonal imbalances, and psychological stress.

Before we move into what to do, we need to examine some fallacies around exercise as the solution to being sedentary that current exist.

The Science of Movement

Many people believe that if they exercise in the morning, or after work, they can be sedentary the rest of the day without consequence. Unfortunately, this is not true. Consistent regular interruptions to sedentary behavior are vital for long-term health. Movement acts as a form of physiological regulation that affects circulation, hormonal balance, and the brain's ability to focus and adapt to stress.[4]

The good news is that you don't need to run marathons or spend hours at the gym to experience the benefits of movement. Research shows that brief, consistent movement throughout the day can significantly improve energy, concentration, mood, and overall ability to recover. It's not about doing more but rather about consistent movement.

A study in the *American Journal of Preventive Medicine* aimed to investigate how different patterns of physical activity throughout the day affect energy levels and overall well-being.[5] The researchers divided participants into three groups to observe the impact of varying levels of movement:

- **Group 1:** This group engaged in no exercise and minimal movement throughout the day. They spent the majority of their time seated, without incorporating any physical activity beyond basic daily functions.
- **Group 2:** This group followed a more traditional approach. They performed a morning exercise routine, such as a 30-minute workout, but after that they remained relatively inactive for the rest of the day, sitting for extended periods at work or home.
- **Group 3:** This group did not engage in any formal exercise routines but committed to moving for about 5 minutes every hour. Whether it was stretching, walking or light activity, they ensured that they remained active throughout the day, breaking up long periods of sitting.

At the end of the study, the results were telling (Figure 10.1):

- **Group 1,** who remained largely sedentary, maintained low energy throughout the day. They experienced a steady decline in alertness and focus, as their bodies were not receiving the regular movement they needed to maintain vitality.
- **Group 2,** despite starting the day with a boost of energy from their morning workout, experienced a sharp drop in energy by midday. Their energy levels resembled those of group 1 as the day progressed, showing that a single burst of exercise in the morning was not enough to sustain energy throughout the day when not followed by movement.
- **Group 3,** the group that incorporated small amounts of movement (3–5 minutes) every hour, had the most consistent and sustained energy throughout the day. By taking regular breaks to move they prevented the afternoon slump that typically affects those who are sedentary.

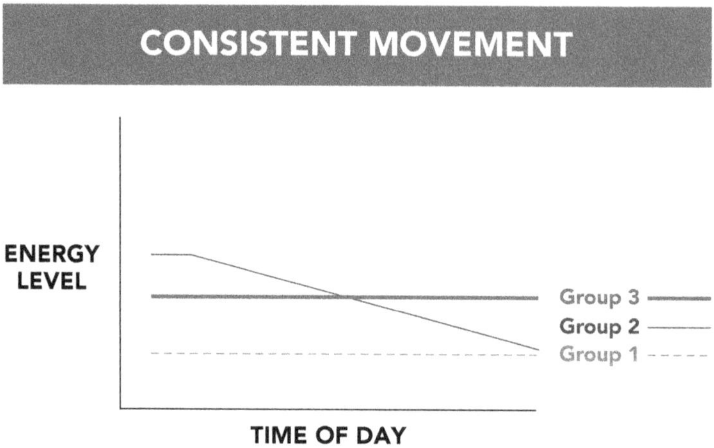

Figure 10.1 Consistent movement during the day maintains energy levels.

This study highlights the significant benefits of regular movement, even in small doses. It emphasizes that while a single workout session may give an initial boost, it is the consistent and frequent movement throughout the day that leads to sustained energy and well-being. Small, manageable habits such as walking for a few minutes or stretching hourly can have a profound impact on our daily energy levels and overall health.

Critical Insight from the Classroom

We see this pattern in room after room—especially in the highest-pressure environments.

Investment bank traders. Military analysts. Senior operators in mission-critical roles. People whose jobs genuinely require long stretches at a desk, eyes on screens, monitoring constantly shifting information.

There is an operational reality they all share:

"Being away from the desk isn't possible for long periods of time."
And in many cases, that's true.
But here's where the trap appears.

When we ask about movement, many participants quickly point to their daily workout.

"I train at 6 a.m."
"I hit the gym hard after work."
"I run five miles before my shift."

And those are positive behaviors. No question.

But then we dig a little deeper.

Once the workout is complete, movement is mentally "banked." They've checked the box. For the remaining 8–12 hours of the day, they're largely stationary—sitting, staring, absorbing stress, rarely standing or shifting posture.

It's almost as if the morning workout gives them permission to be still for the rest of the day.

This is where the misunderstanding lies.

A single, set-piece workout does not cancel out prolonged immobility. From a physiological perspective, extended sitting—especially under cognitive stress—carries its own load. Circulation slows. Muscles remain contracted in static positions. Breathing becomes shallow. The lymphatic system, which depends heavily on movement to function efficiently, stagnates.

And when cognitive stress is layered on top of physical stillness, the body remains in low-grade activation with very little opportunity for regulation.

(*continued*)

(*continued*)

We often hear, "But I trained hard this morning."

That's excellent. But training hard and moving consistently throughout the day serve different purposes.

One builds fitness.

The other supports regulation.

Movement isn't just about calories burned or miles logged. It's about sending the body signals of safety, rhythm, and circulation throughout the day. Small, frequent shifts in posture. Standing during a call. A two-minute calf pump. A quick stretch between tasks. Walking to refill water instead of scrolling.

The story that movement only "counts" when you step fully away from the desk is extremely limiting—and often inaccurate.

We've seen traders who feel chained to their screens begin incorporating 60-second resets between trades. Analysts who can't leave their post build micro-movement into task transitions. The shift isn't dramatic. It's strategic.

The good news is that this trap is easy to overcome once you stop fueling the story that movement requires a gym, a run or a long break.

It requires intention. But you don't need to abandon the desk for 30 minutes.

When you redefine movement as something that can be layered into the day in small, consistent doses, you stop letting the workout serve as an excuse for immobility.

And your nervous system—and performance—respond accordingly.

Activity: Plot Your Daily Movement

To better understand your daily movement habits, take a moment to engage with the movement graph that follows (Figure 10.2). You'll notice the vertical axis representing the duration of movement, ranging from 0 to 60 minutes, while the horizontal axis spans

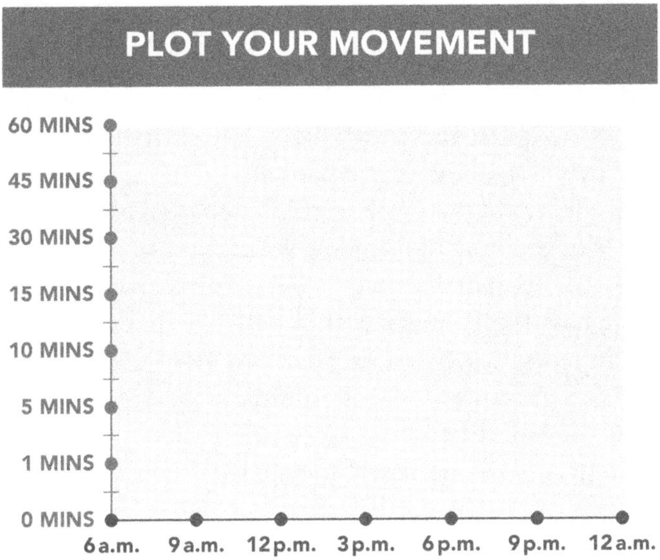

Figure 10.2 Plot your movement on the average day.

from 6 a.m. to midnight, allowing you to track your movement throughout the day.

Start by mapping out your typical day, marking when and how long you engage in any form of movement. This could include anything from walking, stretching, or even standing up during phone calls. Once you've charted this out, take a step back and ask yourself:

What is my graph telling me about my movement throughout the day?

___

___

___

What, if any, movements do I choose that help to decrease stress while maintaining my focus?

___

___

___

For many people this exercise reveals long stretches of inactivity, whether it's sitting at a desk, watching TV or being stuck in traffic, that can drain energy and build up stress. These extended periods without movement can also contribute to physical discomfort, mental fatigue, and overall feelings of stagnation.

As you reflect on your pattern, think about areas where there are opportunities to get more movement. Where can you add short, intentional breaks to incorporate more movement into your day?

What we have experienced as the challenge that most participants have is not in recognizing that they need to move more, but in understanding which movements require minimal disruption to their routine and have the most benefit.

That is where we focus next. Starting with your calf muscles.

The Calf Muscle: Your Second Heart

The calf muscles are often referred to as your "second heart" because they play a crucial role in helping pump blood back toward your chest.[6] This process is vital for maintaining good circulation throughout the body. However, when you remain sedentary for long periods, this natural process of blood circulation slows down. As a result, blood can pool in your lower legs, leading to discomfort, fatigue, and potentially more serious health risks.[7] As we already mentioned, sitting for extended periods can have significant health consequences. To counteract this, incorporating regular movement into your routine, such as calf raises, is crucial to maintaining healthy circulation and reducing these risks.[8]

If this seems too simple, that's because it is. Everyone is likely able to do calf raises, and the benefits of this micro movement practice on body, mind, and even emotions are supported by science. For those who sit for extended periods, it's beneficial to set a timer to remind yourself to do a set of calf raises or foot pumps every hour. This consistent action will help combat the negative effects of sitting and improve your circulation.

Calf Raises

- Improve brain function
- Enhance coordination
- Increase neural pathways
- Boost creativity
- Reduce stress and anxiety

Activity: How to Perform Calf Raises

Here's how you perform the calf raises properly:

Stand upright with your feet about hip-width apart. Make sure you're on a flat surface to maintain balance.

- Slowly rise onto your toes by lifting your heels off the ground.
- Hold the raised position for a moment at the top.
- Gently lower your heels back to the floor. This completes one repetition.
- Perform 10–15 calf raises, maintaining a steady pace.
- As you perform the calf raises, notice how your legs feel. You may experience slight soreness or tightness, especially if your calf muscles are underused. This is normal and indicates that these muscles are being activated.

Foot Pumps (Alternative If Standing Is Not Possible)

- If standing is not an option, sit comfortably in a chair with your feet flat on the ground.
- Point your toes forward, then slowly pull them back toward your knees.
- Repeat the movement 10 times per foot. This will engage the muscles in your lower legs and stimulate blood flow.

Injury Modification: Hand Squeeze and Release

If you are experiencing any issues with your feet, ankles, or Achilles tendon that would prohibit you from doing calf raises (sitting or standing), the next best option to it to squeeze your hands tightly (into a fist) and then release. You can do both hands at the same time or one hand at a time.

This is effective because by squeezing and releasing your hands, you are in effect pumping your forearm muscle, which is the anatomical muscle equivalent to your calf muscle.[9]

As with getting the calf muscle active, squeezing and release your hands will stimulate increased blood flow.

Activity: Incorporating Calf Raises into Your Day

List at least one time during your workday where you will get you calf muscles activated. Be specific: When and where will you choose to activate your calf muscles and what movement will you do in order to active them?

____

____

____

Critical Insight from the Classroom

One of the simplest—and most powerful—shifts we see participants make around movement doesn't require stepping away from work.

In fact, it often accelerates it.

Walking meetings.

In high-pressure environments, especially since the rise of Teams and Zoom, it's easy to become completely desk-bound. Back-to-back virtual meetings create the assumption that you must be in front of your screen at all times. Camera on. Posture fixed. Eyes forward. Minimal movement.

By mid-afternoon, many participants haven't stood up in hours.

When we talk about adding more calf-raising movement into the day—the kind that supports circulation and nervous system regulation—the pushback is predictable:

"I don't have time."

"My calendar's full."

"I'm on calls all day."

But then someone inevitably asks a different question:

"Do we actually need to be on camera for this one?"

That's where things start to change.

A large percentage of meetings do not require screen sharing. They don't require slides. They don't require visual cues. They require conversation.

So some participants have begun asking colleagues, "Can we just dial in old school and talk through the agenda?"

The result? Walk-and-talk meetings.

The impact is disproportionate to the effort.

When you walk during a call—even at a moderate pace—you activate the calf muscles, which support circulation and venous return. Blood flow improves. Oxygen delivery to the brain increases. Posture opens. Breathing deepens naturally. All of this supports clearer thinking.

We've had participants report fewer errors when reviewing work output while walking. Others notice that difficult conversations feel less tense when both parties are moving. Cognitive science supports this—bilateral movement can enhance creativity, problem-solving and flexible thinking.

And there's another benefit: movement helps regulate stress.

Instead of stacking sedentary activation on top of cognitive activation, you're giving the nervous system an outlet. You're not taking a break from work. You're layering regulation into it.

(*continued*)

(*continued*)

One participant put it this way: "My walking calls are the most productive part of my day. We get through the agenda faster."

That's the irony. What feels like it might slow things down often speeds them up.

Of course, not every meeting can be done this way. But many can. Especially one-on-ones, check-ins, brainstorming sessions, alignment conversations.

The key shift is questioning the assumption that effective work requires being glued to a screen.

When you replace even a few static virtual meetings with walk-and-talks, you increase movement, support recovery, and often elevate the quality of the conversation—all without adding a single extra minute to your day.

Sometimes the most powerful recovery tools aren't separate from work.

They're woven directly into it.

Cross-Lateral Movements

The next specific type of movement that we recommend you consistently incorporate into your day are cross-lateral movements. These involve any type of movement that crosses over the midline (middle) of your body. For example, simply reaching your right hand across your body to touch your left shoulder (or vice versa) is a cross-lateral movement.

These movements are incredibly beneficial for brain function, posture, physical coordination, and can help decrease the physiological impact of stress.[10] These movements are extremely impactful because they engage both hemispheres of your brain, by strengthening the connective tissue between the hemispheres called the corpus callosum.[11] The stronger that connective tissue is, the more effectively the right hemisphere "talks" with the left hemisphere, especially when experiencing stress.

Cross-Lateral Movement

- Improves brain function
- Enhances coordination and balance
- Increases neural pathways
- Boosts creativity
- Reduces stress and anxiety

Recommended Cross-Lateral Movements

The Self Hug

Gently cross your arms over each other so that you right hand is on your left shoulder and your left hand is on your right shoulder. To give yourself a self hug you are simply going to rub up and down your arms from your shoulders through your elbows and back up to your shoulders. Repeat this self hug for at 8–10 repetitions.

When you are done, notice how you feel. Our training participants often report that they feel "lighter" or "tingly."

Why Is That?

By crossing your arms you are engaging in a cross-lateral movement the benefits of which we have discussed. The calming aspect of the movement comes from the touch component, which stimulates a specific type of fiber (C-tactile) in the skin.[12] Touching these fibers stimulates the release of neurotransmitters like serotonin and oxytocin, while at the same time slowing your brain waves down to delta level (0.5–4 Hz), which mimics your brain waves when you are about to fall asleep. Consistent practice of this movement will result in better mood, reduced rumination on negative thoughts, and enhance emotional regulation.

Research on the Self Hug

Similar to a traditional hug, the soothing touch of the self hug activates the parasympathetic nervous system (safety signal), countering the sympathetic "fight-or-flight" response (danger signal) associated with stress. Studies have shown that this leads to significant reductions in energy hormones like cortisol, decreased heart rate, lowered blood pressure, and improved immune function through oxytocin release.[13] The safety signal from the self hug leads to increased feelings of relaxation and reduces muscle tension, panic attacks, and sleep disturbances.

Studies indicate that even brief applications can yield immediate and sustained benefits. One study involving healthcare professionals showed improved work performance and reduced absenteeism due to anxiety or depression symptoms persisting up to two months post-session training.[14]

Eye Stretch

Gently place your index and middle finger of your right hand along the infraorbital rim of your left eye (the bony part just below the eye). Then place the palm of your left hand on your left temple. You are going to stretch the fascia around your eye by slowly and gently pulling the skin under your eye down with your right fingers and pulling the skin around your temple up with the palm of your left hand. Hold the stretch for six breaths—breathing at your own comfortable pace. It is important to remember to breathe as you perform this stretch as it helps to reduce tension in and around your eye.

Why It Is Effective

The area under your eyes has tight connective tissue (fascia) that gets stiff from stress, excessive screen time, or holding emotions like worry, frustration, or overwhelm. When you do the eye stretch combined with slow breathing, it loosens that fascia, which sends the safety signal to your brain and nervous system. As a result, your heart rate slows, breathing deepens, and muscle tension decreases. Our training participants report that their mind "slows down," and they experience an increase in their ability to focus almost instantly.

Research on the Eye Stretch

What this eye stretch does is initiate what is referred to as the oculocardiac reflex (OCR). Specifically, the stretch stimulates the trigeminal nerve, which connects to the vagus nerve (your body's primary "relax" nerve).[15] The vagus nerve then tells your heart to slow down and blood pressure to decrease. As a result, this reflex calms your body, reduces anxiety, panic, or overwhelm quickly and efficiently while at the same time allowing you to remain focused.[16]

Reverse Toe Tap

To perform a reverse toe tap, stand with your feet hip-width apart and your hands on your hips for balance. Shift your weight onto your right foot, slightly bend at your right knee while lifting your left foot off the ground. Extend your left leg straight back behind your right leg and tap your toes on the floor. Then return your left leg to the starting position. Repeat with your right leg going behind your left leg and tapping your toes. That is one round. Aim to do at least 10 rounds.

Research on the Reverse Toe Tap

Research suggests that the reverse toe tap effectively strengthens the feet and ankles by targeting muscles like the plantar flexors and improving proprioception, which is crucial for individuals with sedentary lifestyles who experience muscle weakening from prolonged sitting. A systematic review and meta-analysis found that ankle and foot exercises, including those involving toe tapping and balance challenges, significantly enhance ankle strength, flexibility, and overall stability in older adults, reducing fall risk by up to 23% through better force transfer and control during daily movements.[17]

More Simple Ways to Add Movement

You don't need special equipment or a significant time commitment to incorporate more movement into your day. Simple adjustments to your routine can make a big difference in how you feel. Here are a few more easy and effective ways to add movement to your day:

- **Take a 3–5 minute walk every hour:** This doesn't require much effort, but it's incredibly effective. A brief walk around the office or even just stretching your legs stimulates circulation and activates your calf muscles. Not only does this give your mind and body a break from sitting, it also brings many of the same benefits as calf raises and is also a cross-lateral movement.

- **Stand during phone calls or meetings:** Whenever possible, stand up while talking on the phone or in meetings. Standing activates more muscles, improves posture and helps keep your energy levels higher. If you're not able to stand the whole time, alternate between sitting and standing to avoid long periods of stillness.
- **Do toe taps while sitting at your desk:** While seated, take the opportunity to stretch your arms, legs, or torso. Even simple actions like toe taps can help. These movements keep your body engaged and prevent the stiffness that can come from staying in one position for too long. Again, you engage your calf muscles when doing toe taps.
- **Fascial Maneuvers:** These are easy to perform rotational movements that can be done sitting or standing and are extremely effective at inducing the safety signal in the body. These movements allow the body to release and increase focus simultaneously. You can learn more about these movements by searching the YouTube channel of Human Garage.

These small shifts are more than just good habits. They send powerful signals to your brain and body that it's okay to release tension, reduce stress, and replenish your energy. By consistently moving throughout your day, you'll feel more focused, energized and ready to tackle whatever comes your way.

Reflection Activity: Your Movement Plan

Take a moment to reflect on your daily routine and think about ways you can incorporate more movement into your life. Let's dive into a simple exercise that can help you identify both opportunities and challenges when it comes to adding movement to your day.

Consider the moments throughout your day where you could build in small, simple movements. This could be as easy as taking a brisk walk after lunch, opting for the stairs instead of the elevator or even stretching while waiting for your coffee to brew. These opportunities don't need to take any extra time out of your day, just a small shift in how you approach certain tasks. Use the examples we've shared as inspiration and explore your own ideas that fit naturally into your routine.

Think about your daily schedule and write down a few specific opportunities where you could add movement. The more concrete and actionable your opportunities are, the easier it will be to stick to them. Be specific about the time of day, the type of movement and where it fits into your routine. For example, you may decide to take a 5-minute walk right after your morning meeting. The more specificity the brain gets, the easier it is to implement the new behavior.

When are opportunities to add more movement to your day?

____

____

____

It's important to identify what could be getting in the way of adding more movement into your routine. Be honest with yourself about the challenges you face, whether they're physical, mental, or situational. Do you find it difficult to get started? Do you forget to move when you're in the flow of work? Are you often too tired to move after a long day?

For example, you might realize that:

- "I forget to stand up when I'm deeply immersed in work."
- "I'm usually too tired after a busy day to think about moving."
- "I feel self-conscious about doing exercises at work."
- "I have back pain that makes me avoid movement sometimes."

Identifying these barriers helps you understand what's stopping you from moving more. It's important to recognize these obstacles so that you can actively work on overcoming them.

What barriers might prevent you from moving more?

____

____

____

Once you've identified your barriers, think of creative ways to overcome them. This is where you get to be resourceful. Maybe setting reminders or creating a system could help. Perhaps breaking up your movement into shorter, more manageable sessions could make it feel less overwhelming. For example:

- "Set an hourly timer on my phone to remind me to stand and stretch."
- "Place a sticky note on my computer screen to prompt me to take a walk after every two hours of work."
- "Start my day with a 5-minute stretch routine so I'm more energized and less likely to skip movement."
- "Find a space where I can do discreet stretches without feeling self-conscious."

By creating specific strategies, you make it easier to overcome the obstacles that could prevent you from moving more. The key is consistency, and small adjustments will eventually become a habit.

What specific strategies can you use to overcome those barriers?

____

____

____

Critical Insight from the Classroom

In many of our sessions, we ask a simple question:

> "Do you have a standing desk?"
> More and more hands go up.

Then we follow with the second question:

> "Do you ever actually use it in the standing position?"
> That's when the laughter starts.
> More often than not, the answer is no.

It's not because people don't believe standing is beneficial. Most are aware that prolonged sitting isn't ideal. It's not because they don't have the equipment. They've invested in the adjustable desk. It's sitting right there.

It's because we get used to working in a certain way.

Habits are powerful. Once your body and brain associate "work mode" with sitting, that becomes the default. The desk may be adjustable, but behavior isn't automatic just because the option exists. Without a cue, we forget the alternative is even available.

In one workshop, a participant shared a simple but brilliant solution.

She said, "What if I asked the cleaning staff to move everyone's desk into the standing position at night?"

The room paused.

"So when we come in the next morning," she continued, "the default is standing. If we want to sit, we lower it. But at least we start standing."

That small idea reframed the entire conversation.

Instead of relying on willpower during the busiest part of the day, she changed the starting point. The environment would now cue the behavior.

Others quickly built on it.

"At home," someone added, "I could raise my desk as the last act of my workday. Put it in my calendar. That way, tomorrow morning it's already set to standing."

That's the insight.

Behavior change often doesn't fail because we lack knowledge. It fails because we lack cues.

We know standing intermittently during the day supports circulation, reduces prolonged static posture, and can help maintain energy. But without a prompt, the old pattern wins.

By shifting the default—raising the desk at night instead of hoping to remember in the morning—you remove friction. Now sitting becomes the deliberate act, not standing.

(*continued*)

(continued)

This aligns with what behavioral science consistently shows: environment shapes action more than intention does. A subtle cue can make the difference between "I should" and "I did."

The standing desk itself isn't the breakthrough. The cue is.

Sometimes we don't need a new strategy. We just need a small environmental nudge that reminds us to use the tools we already have—in ways that serve us better.

These reflections help you connect to the larger goal of integrating movement into your daily routine in a way that feels both natural and doable. When you start to identify where movement fits in and how to overcome your barriers, you'll find yourself feeling more energized, focused and able to take on the day with more ease.

Keep in mind that any movement you do that is not harmful to you is good movement.

In the next chapter, we're going to focus on a topic that may actually be the primary stressor in your life: hydration. . .specifically, the lack thereof. Surprisingly, the solution is not as simple as "drink more water," which we will discuss.

11

Hydrating Your Way to Increased Energy

WATER IS THE lifeblood of our existence, the foundation of every bodily function, and a cornerstone of vibrant health. Comprising 60–70% of our body, water is essential for delivering nutrients, regulating temperature, lubricating joints, and facilitating the electrical signals that drive our nervous system.[1] Yet, many of us are chronically dehydrated, not because we don't drink water, but because our bodies struggle to absorb and retain it effectively. Dehydration, even at subtle levels, can manifest as fatigue, brain fog, joint pain, digestive issues, and even emotional imbalances.[2]

The brain, which accounts for only about 2% of body weight but consumes roughly 20% of the body's total energy, is particularly vulnerable to these effects. Proper hydration and mineralization ensure the efficient transport of glucose and oxygen to brain cells, sustaining mental performance and preventing the energy dips that hinder focus and productivity. This chapter explores the art and science of hydration, offering practical recommendations and best practices to help you maintain consistent hydration, optimize your body's fluid dynamics, and unlock your potential for energy, clarity, and resilience.

Understanding Hydration and Dehydration

As we mentioned, hydration is more than just drinking water; it's about ensuring your body can absorb and utilize that water effectively. The human body is designed to thrive when properly hydrated, but our modern lifestyles—marked by processed foods, stress, and sedentary habits—disrupt this balance. As a result, research suggests that up to 82% of people may be chronically dehydrated, not due to a lack of water intake but because their bodies lack the minerals needed to hold onto water.[2]

This is a very important point. Because most people we work with are drinking enough water. However, without adequate sodium, potassium, magnesium, and other trace minerals, that water passes through the body without nourishing cells (it actually "steals" the existing minerals in the body) leading to a large variety of symptoms like digestive issues, skin issues, chronic pain, allergies, fatigue, brain fog, irritability. . .and so on.[3]

What do all of those issues have in common? They increase stress in the body.

Dehydration isn't always obvious. While thirst is a common signal, it often appears late, after the body is already struggling. Subtle signs—dry lips, stiff joints, low energy, or difficulty focusing—can indicate that your body's water balance is off.[4] Chronic dehydration may also weaken the body's ability to carry electrical signals through its connective tissues, impairing communication between nerves, glands, and organs.[5] This is especially critical for brain-based activities, where mental tasks demand high energy expenditure. The brain relies on a steady supply of hydrated, mineral-balanced fluids to maintain neurotransmitter function and ATP production—the cellular energy source that powers cognition, decision-making, and sustained attention.[6] Without optimal hydration, mental performance suffers, leading to reduced efficiency in tasks requiring concentration or creativity. To counter this, we must approach hydration holistically, combining water intake with mineral-rich foods, mindful movement, and an understanding of how water interacts with our body's systems.[7]

Critical Insight from the Classroom

The classroom is an unexpectedly revealing place to observe hydration habits.

Without fail, we tend to see two distinct groups.

The first group walks in carrying large water bottles or flasks. Stainless steel. Measured markings on the side. Sometimes electrolytes already mixed in. These participants have clearly built accessibility into their routine. Water is within arm's reach at all times. They sip consistently throughout the session without needing prompts.

Hydration, for them, is a system—not an afterthought.

The second group is just as interesting.

They don't bring water with them. But when we place glasses on the tables and fill them up, they drink. If we refill the glasses, they drink again. The behavior is there—but only when cued.

Here's what's fascinating.

Once the glass is empty, it often sits in front of them for hours. Right there. In plain sight. But unnoticed. No one asks for a refill. No one gets up to replenish it.

It's a perfect example of a "hiding in plain sight" blind spot.

These participants are not resistant to hydration. They simply don't have reliable cues built into their daily routine. In the classroom, we are the cue. Outside the classroom, that structure disappears—and so does consistent intake.

This small observation tells a much bigger story.

Hydration isn't just about knowledge. Almost everyone knows they "should" drink more water. It's about environment and habit loops. The first group has engineered accessibility. The second group relies on external prompts.

Both groups, however, have something to refine.

The first group—the heavy water carriers—are generally in a good place from a habit standpoint. But there's a subtle

(*continued*)

(*continued*)

consideration here. Constantly chugging large volumes of plain water without attention to electrolytes can dilute minerals over time, especially for those who are training hard, sweating regularly, or drinking excessively in response to stress. Hydration isn't just volume—it's balance.

The second group's opportunity is different.

They need cues.

That might mean keeping a bottle on their desk. Setting calendar reminders. Pairing water with existing behaviors—every meeting start, every email block, every bathroom break. The goal is to shift from reactive hydration ("when someone fills my glass") to proactive hydration ("I built this into my day").

The classroom becomes a mirror.

You can see who has engineered the environment to support the behavior and who is depending on external structure.

Hydration may seem small, but it's foundational. Even mild dehydration can affect focus, mood, and perceived stress levels. If you want to operate closer to your Best Self, basic physiological inputs matter.

Sometimes the lesson isn't in what people say.

It's in the empty glass sitting quietly in front of them.

"Eat Your Water": A Natural Approach to Hydration

Though drinking water is absolutely necessary for your health, it is our perspective that simply drinking water is not the most effective way to remain hydrated.

The most effective way to hydrate is to "eat your water" by consuming foods naturally rich in water and electrolytes.[8] Fruits and vegetables like cucumbers (96% water), watermelon (92% water), celery (95% water), zucchini (94% water), and leafy greens (90–95% water) deliver hydration in a form that the body can readily use.[9] These foods release water slowly during digestion, providing a steady source of hydration while supplying critical minerals like potassium and magnesium that enhance water retention in your cells.[10] Unlike plain water, which can sometimes flush through the system too quickly, thereby actually depleting your body's minerals, water-rich foods support sustained hydration and nourish the body with fiber and nutrients.

Incorporating water-rich foods into your diet offers multiple benefits. The slow release of water supports digestion and prevents the dilution of electrolytes, while the fiber in these foods helps regulate fluid balance. This approach transforms hydration into a nourishing, enjoyable part of your meals, making it easier to maintain consistency. Moreover, these foods contribute to energy stability by providing bioavailable minerals that aid in glucose metabolism, ensuring both the brain and body have the fuel needed for prolonged mental and physical performance.

The Critical Role of Minerals

Minerals are the key to unlocking water's potential in the body. Sodium, in particular, is essential for water absorption, acting as a gatekeeper that allows cells to retain fluids.[11] Without sufficient sodium, drinking large amounts of water can lead to overhydration, where the body flushes out water and electrolytes, leaving you dehydrated despite high fluid intake. This is especially common among athletes who drink excessive water without replenishing minerals, stripping their bodies of the resources needed to maintain balance. Potassium, magnesium, and calcium also play vital roles, supporting muscle function, nerve signaling, and fluid regulation.

These minerals are indispensable for energy production and sustaining human performance. Magnesium, for example, acts as a cofactor in over 300 enzymatic reactions, including the synthesis of ATP, the body's primary energy molecule.[12] Potassium and sodium facilitate the sodium-potassium pump, which generates electrical gradients essential for nerve impulses and muscle contractions—processes that consume significant energy in both the brain and body.

In mental activities, proper mineralization ensures efficient synaptic transmission, reducing the energy cost of cognition and preventing fatigue during tasks like problem-solving or learning.

Modern diets often lack these essential minerals due to reliance on processed foods and mineral-depleted soils.[13] To optimize hydration, focus on mineral-rich foods. Adding a pinch of high-quality, unrefined sea salt to your water or meals can enhance water retention and provide trace minerals that support overall health.[14,15] For example, a glass of water with a dash of sea salt and a squeeze of lemon can be a simple, effective way to boost hydration and replenish electrolytes, especially after exercise or in hot climates, while also supporting the energy demands of daily mental and physical activities.

The Power of Structured Water

Not all water is created equal. The way water is structured at a molecular level can influence how effectively the body absorbs it.[16] Water in its natural state—found in springs or within the cells of plants and animals—has a unique molecular arrangement that makes it more bioavailable. This "structured" water is thought to carry electrical signals more efficiently through the body's connective tissues, enhancing cellular communication and hydration.[17] You can mimic this by gently stirring water to create a vortex, exposing it to sunlight, or storing it in glass containers, which may help align its molecular structure and improve its interaction with your cells.

While the science of structured water is still emerging, simple practices can enhance the quality of the water you consume. Avoid plastic bottles, which can leach chemicals that disrupt the body's chemistry, and opt for filtered water stored in glass or stainless steel. Experiment with swirling your water or leaving it in sunlight for a few minutes before drinking to potentially improve its bioavailability. These small steps can complement your hydration routine, making every sip more effective, and may even support better energy transfer at the cellular level, benefiting both brain function and overall vitality.

Hydration and Movement

Hydration and movement are deeply interconnected. The body's connective tissues, particularly the fascia, act as a network that distributes water and nutrients throughout the body.[18] When we engage in functional movements—those that mimic natural activities like squatting, climbing, or twisting—we stimulate the fascia, promoting fluid circulation and enhancing hydration at a cellular level.[19] This process helps release stored tension and ensures that water reaches deep tissues, supporting everything from joint mobility to emotional balance.

Incorporate 2–3 minutes of simple, functional, cross-lateral, or rotational movements into your daily routine, such as gentle spinal twists, arm swings, or reverse toe taps. These movements not only improve physical alignment but also enhance the body's ability to absorb and utilize water. For example, gentle rotational movements release tension in the spine, allowing water and nutrients to circulate more freely throughout your body. By improving blood flow and lymphatic drainage, movement also delivers hydrated, oxygen-rich blood to the brain, fueling its high energy requirements and sustaining mental performance during demanding cognitive tasks. By pairing hydration with movement, you create a synergistic effect that amplifies your body's ability to consistently release stress and signal "safety" more often.

Best Practices for Consistent Hydration

To make hydration a seamless part of your life, adopt these practical strategies:

- **Begin with Intention:** Start your day by hydrating either through food or mineralized water, adding a pinch of unrefined sea salt or a splash of lemon juice to enhance absorption. This replenishes fluids lost overnight immediately lowering your body's experience of stress.
- **Prioritize Water-Rich Foods:** Include water-rich fruits and/or vegetables in every snack or meal.
- **Replenish Minerals:** Ensure adequate sodium, potassium, and magnesium intake ideally through foods rich in those minerals.
- **Sip Consistently:** Drink water steadily throughout the day rather than gulping large amounts at once. Carry a reusable glass or stainless steel bottle and take small sips every 15–30 minutes to maintain steady hydration.

- **Enhance Water Quality:** Use filtered water stored in glass or stainless steel containers. Experiment with stirring water to create a vortex or exposing it to sunlight to potentially improve its structure and bioavailability.
- **Rotate Your Body:** Perform 2–3 minutes (ideally every hour) of cross-lateral or rotational movements to stimulate fluid circulation and enhance hydration at a cellular level.
- **Minimize Dehydrating Factors:** Limit caffeine, alcohol, and processed foods, which can deplete fluids and minerals. When consuming these, balance them with extra mineralized water and electrolyte-rich foods.

These practices not only support physical endurance but also bolster the brain's energy needs, ensuring sustained focus and resilience in high-performance scenarios.

Overcoming Hydration Challenges

Staying hydrated can be challenging in busy or demanding environments. If drinking water feels monotonous, infuse it with mineral rich foods that enhance the flavor and mineral content of the water (e.g., cucumber or citrus) to make it more appealing.

Set reminders on your phone or keep a water bottle visible to prompt regular sips. If you're drinking ample water but still feel dehydrated, the answer is not to just drink more water. It is to focus on increasing your mineral intake, through hydrating foods, or a high-quality electrolyte supplement. In dry climates, high altitudes, or during intense physical activity, increase water and mineral consumption to compensate for greater fluid loss.

From our perspective, proper hydration is the cornerstone of managing stress more effectively because not getting the required amount of water into your cells will, directly or indirectly, have a negative impact on literally every other part of your brain and body.

Therefore, the first area you need to focus on to manage stress more effectively is proper hydration.

By eating water-rich foods, prioritizing minerals, enhancing water quality, incorporating functional movement, and building a consistent routine, you can transform hydration into a powerful practice not just for managing stress, but for your overall health and vitality. This holistic approach ensures that both your brain and body receive the energy necessary to sustain peak performance, whether in mental endeavors or physical challenges.

Activity: Your Hydration Plan

As we mentioned, we strongly recommend that you get your mineral levels checked through blood work (order a full mineral panel). If you are low on certain minerals, drinking a lot of water can actually make things worse. When we consume too much water without proper mineral balance, it flows through the body and can begin to draw out minerals, similarly to how water slowly erodes rock along a shoreline.

In addition to formal bloodwork analysis, it is vital for you to learn how to connect more deeply with your body and understand its unique needs. That may sound a bit woo-woo, it's not, it is actually quite simple to start training yourself to do.

Here is how you do it.

When incorporating new practices such as hourly hydration or certain movement exercises, always ask yourself these three guiding questions:

1. Is it working for me?
2. Is it sustainable?
3. Is it consistently providing me the energy I need to be my best?

Use your answers to inform and refine your choices moving forward. Pay particular attention to how these practices affect your mental energy and performance, as balanced hydration directly supports the brain's high demands for sustained focus and creativity.

Lastly, when it comes to hydration, the most beneficial practice to engage in is what is called "habit stacking." This means pairing a new habit, like hydrating every hour, with an existing behavior such as checking your phone or going to the bathroom.

What are your opportunities to pair hydration with an activity you are already doing?

____

____

____

If we were forced to choose just one strategy to make sure that everyone who reads this book would implement every day, it is to consistently hydrate yourself. Hydration literally impacts every aspect of your body's functioning and is absolutely critical in order for you to manage stress more effectively.

Next we're going to focus on the movement all of us engage in every moment, breathing, and how modern life has subtly led our breathing patterns to become restricted.

12

Breathing Your Way to Calm and Focused

Every moment of your life, your breath is working for or against you, yet it's something you rarely think about. When stress strikes, your breath often becomes shallow and rapid, signaling danger to your body. But here's the good news: your breath isn't just a bystander in your stress response, it's a primary tool you can use to regain control.

Conscious, balanced breathing is one of the simplest and fastest ways to shift your body from a state of stress (fight-or-flight) to a state of calm (rest and digest).[1] It's a built-in reset button for your nervous system. Your breath is directly connected to your nervous system. When you're stressed, your brain sends signals to your body to prepare for danger. These signals cause an increased heart rate, shallow rapid breathing, and muscle tension. This response is helpful in a life-threatening situation, but when it happens because of an email or a tense meeting, it drains your energy unnecessarily.

On the flip side, slow, intentional breathing sends a "safety" signal to your brain, activating your parasympathetic nervous system.[2] This reduces your heart rate, relaxes your muscles, and brings you back to a state of clarity and focus.[3]

Breathing is one of the most fundamental and powerful functions of the body, yet most of us are unaware that we may not be breathing properly. In this chapter, we will explore the incredible impact your breath has on cellular health. Proper breathing is essential for two key processes: delivering oxygen to every cell and removing carbon dioxide, a waste product of cellular energy production. When breathing is optimized, it ensures your body's energy systems function at their best. However, many of us are unknowingly limiting our breath's potential.

In this chapter, we'll explore how Balanced Brain Breathing can support physical and mental calm. You'll also find simple tools and exercises to help you tap into the power of your breath and enhance your overall well-being.

The Problem for Most People: Unconscious Restrictive Breathing

Here is the issue with breathing. Most, if not all of us, are not breathing properly throughout the day. And often, we do not even realize it.

When the body is under stress, breathing becomes restrictive. This means your breath becomes quick, shallow, and often disconnected. It is a natural response. Think of a time when you were watching a scary movie. As the tension builds and the villain suddenly appears, what happens? You hold your breath. Your body freezes, even if only for a second. This is your nervous system reacting to a perceived threat. It is an automatic attempt to regroup, prepare and protect.

Now consider how often this same reaction is triggered throughout your day. It might happen when an unexpected email pops up, when you get a last minute request, or when your phone buzzes with a message. These moments may seem small, but your body often treats them like little alarms. With each one, you subtly hold or shorten your breath, over and over again.

Without awareness, this becomes your default pattern. And as we have said before, any thought, feeling, or behavior that you repeat, you are training into a habit. In this case, you're training your body to live in a restricted breathing state, even when there is no real danger present.

Healthy breathing should be slow and steady. Ideally, you would take about six full breaths every minute. This would look like a five-second inhale followed by a five-second exhale. This rhythm supports calm, clarity, and energy.

When you are breathing restrictively, you might be taking 15 to 20 shallow breaths per minute. This keeps the body in a chronic state of low-level hyperventilation.[4] It increases feelings of stress and anxiety and reinforces the very state you may be trying to escape.

Learning to recognize this pattern is powerful. By becoming aware of your breath and gently shifting it back to a slower, fuller rhythm, you give your body the signal that it is safe. You interrupt the stress response and return to a space of ease and inner harmony.

Consequences of Restrictive Breathing

Restrictive or shallow breathing can have a wide range of negative effects on both your mind and body (Figure 12.1). One of the most immediate consequences is reduced oxygen intake. Shallow breaths primarily fill only the upper part of the lungs, which have less surface area for gas exchange. As a result, less oxygen reaches the alveoli, the tiny air sacs where oxygen is transferred into the bloodstream. This leads to decreased oxygen availability in the body and especially the brain, resulting in symptoms such as mental fog, fatigue, and difficulty concentrating.[5]

On a neurological level, shallow breathing can disrupt brainwave patterns. Brain coherence, meaning the coordinated and harmonious activity of brainwaves, is associated with focus, emotional equilibrium,

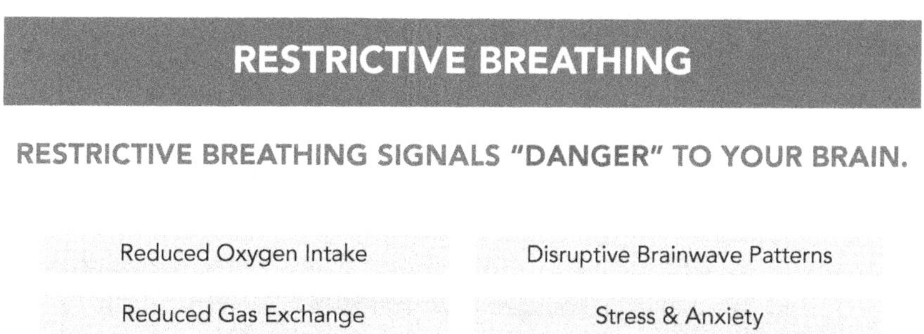

Figure 12.1 Consequences of chronic restrictive breathing.

and a general sense of well-being. When breathing becomes rapid and shallow, this coherence is disturbed, which can hinder cognitive function and make emotional regulation more difficult.

In addition, shallow breathing reinforces the body's stress response. It tells the nervous system that something is wrong, increasing feelings of anxiety and making it harder to return to a state of calm. Over time, this pattern can contribute to chronic stress and heightened sensitivity to everyday challenges.

At the cellular level, restricted breathing affects the delivery of oxygen throughout the body. Less oxygen is loaded onto hemoglobin, the protein in red blood cells responsible for transporting oxygen. Since cells rely on oxygen to produce energy through cellular respiration, any limitation in oxygen supply can impair cellular function. This may manifest as low energy, dizziness, and reduced cognitive performance.

In short, how you breathe has a profound impact on your clarity, calm, and capacity. Bringing awareness to your breath is not just a wellness practice. It is a fundamental act of support for every cell in your body.

Balanced Brain Breathing

A simple yet powerful technique for calming the nervous system while enhancing mental clarity and focus is Balanced Brain Breathing. Rooted in ancient yogic practices, particularly a form of pranayama known as Nadi Shodhana, this technique has been adapted to support modern wellness and cognitive performance.[6]

The practice involves gently alternating your breath between the left and right nostrils, using your fingers to close one nostril at a time while maintaining a smooth, steady breath. This rhythmic switching is believed to support communication between the two hemispheres of the brain by stimulating the corpus callosum, the bundle of nerve fibers connecting the left and right sides.[7] When breathing alternates from nostril to nostril, it engages both hemispheres in a rhythmic and balanced way. This can promote greater brain coherence, improve emotional regulation, and enhance mental clarity, as the brain begins to function in a more integrated and harmonious state.

How Does It Work?

The breath directly influences the nervous system. Breathing through the left nostril activates the parasympathetic nervous system, which promotes calm and relaxation. Breathing through the right nostril stimulates the sympathetic nervous system, associated with alertness and action. By alternating between the two nostrils, this practice gently regulates your internal state, helping you feel centered, clear, and grounded.[8]

In moments of stress, distraction, or overwhelm, the brain often becomes imbalanced and scattered. Balanced Brain Breathing restores stability in your system, allowing you to move from a reactive state to a more responsive one. Just a few minutes of this practice can shift you into a more focused and present state, helping you regain clarity and composure.

Activity: Experience Balanced Brain Breathing

Let's try this practice together:

1. **Posture:** Sit in a comfortable position with your spine upright and your head gently balanced over your shoulders. You can sit in a chair with your back supported or lie down if that feels better. Keep your mouth closed throughout the practice and breathe only through your nose.
2. **Ventilation Breaths (×3):** Begin with three deep, full breaths through both nostrils. This helps prepare your body and mind for the practice:
   - Inhale deeply through your nose, filling your lungs completely.
   - Exhale slowly and fully through your nose and mouth. As you breathe out, gently bend your body slightly forward to help release all the air. Repeat this for a total of three breaths, keeping your breathing comfortable and without strain.
3. **Hand Positions:** You will use your right hand to gently close your right nostril with your thumb. And you will use your right index finger to gently close your left nostril. You will alternate between nostrils during the practice (not closing both nostrils at the same time).

4. **Begin the Breathing Cycle:**
   - Exhale completely through your left nostril.
   - Inhale slowly and deeply through your left nostril. Take a smooth, comfortable breath. Do not force or strain.
5. **Switch Nostrils:**
   - Close your left nostril with your right ring finger and lift your right thumb to open your right nostril.
   - Exhale completely through your right nostril.
   - Inhale slowly and fully through your right nostril.
6. **Continue the Cycle:**
   - Switch nostrils again: Close the right nostril with your thumb, and open the left by lifting your ring finger.
   - Exhale left, inhale left.
   - Switch and repeat: Exhale right, inhale right. Continue this alternating pattern for several minutes, moving at your own pace.
7. **End the Practice:** When finished, release your hand, return to natural breathing through both nostrils, and sit quietly for a moment, noticing how you feel.

Benefits of Balanced Brain Breathing

This technique is especially effective when practiced for just 2–5 minutes once or twice a day. A great time to practice could be first thing in the morning, during a midday break, or before bed. Some of the key benefits of Balanced Brain Breathing include[9]:

- Promotes relaxation and reduces stress
- Improves focus and concentration
- Balances the autonomic nervous system
- Enhances mental clarity and brain function

By incorporating Balanced Brain Breathing into your daily routine, you can cultivate a sense of calm and clarity that helps you navigate even the busiest and most stressful moments with ease. Whether you're preparing for an important event, trying to stay grounded during a hectic day, or simply looking for a moment of peace, this practice provides a simple and effective way to reset your mind and body.

Critical Insight from the Classroom

When we introduce breathwork in the classroom, there's often an unspoken assumption in the room:

"This is great. . . but when would I actually have time to do it?"

Many people believe that regulating their breath requires stepping away from work. Closing the door. Sitting cross-legged. Lighting a candle.

But one of the most important realizations participants have is this:

You don't have to stop working to start breathing intentionally.

Breathing is already happening. The shift is simply bringing awareness and control to it.

We've had participants share that during heated discussions—tense negotiations, difficult feedback conversations, high-stakes meetings—they began subtly shifting their breath. Slowing it. Deepening it. Extending the exhale.

No one else in the room knew they were doing it.

But internally, everything changed.

When you slow and regulate your breath, especially by extending the exhale, you activate the parasympathetic nervous system. Heart rate begins to settle. Emotional reactivity decreases. Cognitive flexibility improves. In other words, you give yourself just enough space between stimulus and response to avoid reacting in a suboptimal way.

One participant told us, "I didn't say the thing I was about to say—just because I focused on my breathing."

That's powerful.

Then we layer in something even more strategic: **predictive breathwork.**

When participants experience the impact of a 2-minute Balanced Brain Breathing exercise, something shifts in how they view their calendar.

(*continued*)

(*continued*)

Instead of seeing meetings as isolated events, they begin scanning their schedule for what we call "hard pivots."

One participant described her day as two very different worlds. Mornings were filled with group discussions—high energy, collaborative, sometimes chaotic. Afternoons were stacked with one-to-one meetings requiring presence, listening, and emotional nuance.

The transition between those blocks was tough. She often carried the intensity of the morning into the first afternoon conversation, which affected the quality of those one-to-ones.

Her solution?

She plugged in a 2-minute Balanced Brain Breathing reset between the blocks.

Two minutes.

No dramatic overhaul. No lost productivity.

But that deliberate pause allowed her nervous system to recalibrate. She entered the afternoon grounded instead of charged. Present instead of reactive.

That's the shift from reactive living to intentional performance.

Breathwork doesn't need to be a separate activity. It can run quietly in the background during a conversation. And when used predictively—before a known transition—it becomes a performance enhancer.

Small. Intentional. Powerful.

While we often look for big interventions, it's easy to overlook the impact of something as simple as the breath. But the participants who begin using it strategically quickly realize:

You don't need more time.

You need better transitions.

And sometimes, 2 minutes is all it takes to change the trajectory of the next hour.

When is one time of day where you will practice Balanced Brain Breathing for 2 minutes?

____

____

____

Further Breathing Practices

Breathing is one of the most powerful tools we have to influence our mental and physical states. Countless books have been written on the power of the breath and different breathing practices so next to the two mentioned practices there are many more. Below are two more simple yet effective techniques that our training participants report that they actually practice. Remember, there are hundreds of strategies and tactics available. All of them are only useful if you practice them consistently.

Focused Inhale/Exhale

By manipulating the length of your inhale and exhale, you can control your nervous system's response, either calming or activating your body and mind.[10]

- **To calm your system:** Exhale one beat longer than you inhale *(for example: inhale for 4 counts, exhale for 5).*

  This pattern activates your parasympathetic nervous system, helping your body relax and recover. It's perfect for winding down, easing stress, or preparing for rest.
- **To increase alertness:** Inhale one beat longer than you exhale *(for example: inhale for 5 counts, exhale for 4).*

  This stimulates your sympathetic nervous system, increasing energy and focus. Use this technique when you need a mental boost or a quick energy pick-me-up.

With just a few rounds (around 1 to 2 minutes) you'll begin to feel the benefits. Adjust the rhythm to suit your needs, whether you're seeking relaxation or heightened awareness.

1-3-2 Breathing

The 1-3-2 technique involves using multiples to create a balanced breath cycle. This method leverages the power of proportion, allowing you to control the timing of each phase of your breath.

Here's how it works:

- **Inhale** for a set number of seconds (e.g., 3 seconds)
- **Hold** for three times that number (e.g., 9 seconds)
- **Exhale** for twice the original number (e.g., 6 seconds)

Repeat this cycle for at least three rounds. This exercise helps increase alertness by regulating the flow of oxygen and carbon dioxide, which can invigorate your mind and body. The rhythm helps sharpen your focus and heighten clarity.

Breathing Beyond Stress

Breathing is not only effective for managing stress. It also enhances other aspects of life. By practicing conscious breathing regularly, you may start to notice significant improvements. For example, many people experience better sleep quality. Calming breaths before bed help activate the parasympathetic nervous system, signaling to your body that it's time to relax, allowing you to fall asleep faster and enjoy a deeper sleep.

Conscious breathing also improves emotional regulation. Whether you're feeling stressed, frustrated, or overwhelmed, intentional breathing helps you take a moment to pause, center yourself, and respond more thoughtfully. As a result, you become less reactive and better able to handle emotional challenges in a calm and harmonious way.

Moreover, breathing exercises increase coping strength in the face of adversity. Life can be unpredictable, but by regularly practicing mindful breathing, your body learns to return to calmness more easily, even during difficult situations. This ability to stay grounded and clear-headed helps you approach challenges with greater confidence and clarity.

Creating Your Personal Breathing Plan

Now that you've learned how powerful conscious breathing can be, it's time to create a plan to incorporate it into your daily life. Start by reflecting on a few key questions to make it easy, personal, and sustainable.

1. When do I feel most stressed or overwhelmed during the day?

   Think about the specific times or situations that tend to trigger stress for you.

   Example: "During my commute" or "Before a big meeting"

   ____

   ____

   ____

2. When do I naturally have a few quiet minutes?

   Look for moments in your day when you can take a pause. These natural breaks are the perfect opportunities for breathing exercises.

   Example: "Right after waking up" or "Before lunch"

   ____

   ____

   ____

3. Which breathing technique feels most supportive to me?

   There are many effective breathing techniques; start with one that resonates with you and that you will actually do. Choose one technique that feels easy and effective. Keep it simple.

   Example: "Practice Balanced Brain Breathing before meetings."

   ____

   ____

   ____

4. How will I use breathing in moments of stress?

   Once you've identified your stress triggers and the natural pauses in your day, plan how to use breathwork in those moments. The key is to practice consciously and intentionally when stress is building.

   Example: "Practice 1-3-2 breathing for 1 minute before my commute."

   ____

   ____

   ____

Now, using the answers from the questions above, begin to create your own simple breathing plan. Choose a few specific breathing techniques you want to practice regularly and decide on a few key moments in your day to take short breathing breaks, such as before a meeting, after a difficult call, or when transitioning between tasks. If possible, schedule a daily practice of 2 minutes of Balanced Brain Breathing, especially at times when you tend to feel stressed or overwhelmed. Make this plan your own. Focus on what genuinely supports you. The goal is to consistently engage with your breath, your most accessible and reliable tool to support the nervous system. With just a little practice, breathing can become a steady ally, helping you move through the day with greater focus, clarity, and ease.

Even now, pause and simply notice your breath, which will help you feel refreshed and re-centered before reading on.

13

Sleeping Your Way to the Safety Signal

WHAT IS THE one behavior that will recharge your entire system back to 100% ideally?

Yes, sleep.

Sleep is one of the most underestimated tools for healing and recovery, yet it plays a vital role in maintaining mental clarity, emotional balance, and long-term health. While most people understand that sleep is important for energy and focus, few realize that one of its most fundamental functions is detoxification: physical, emotional, and mental.[1]

Purpose of Sleep

During sleep, the brain activates a specialized system called the glymphatic system. This system is responsible for clearing out metabolic waste products, including amyloid-beta and tau proteins, which are associated with neurodegenerative conditions such as Alzheimer's disease.[2] Without sufficient and high-quality sleep, this detox process is impaired, leaving the body and brain in a state of incomplete recovery, thereby putting your body into a danger signal.

Sleep also contributes significantly to brain function. It helps consolidate memories by strengthening new neural pathways.[3] It supports learning and adaptability through a process known as neural plasticity. Sleep restores mental energy and improves focus, creativity, and decision-making.

Scientific evidence confirms that sleep is not just a passive activity, but a critical period of neurological repair and reset (i.e., detoxification from your day).[4] Here are a few additional facts that illustrate its importance:

- One night of poor sleep can significantly reduce emotional regulation and cognitive performance.[5]
- Chronic sleep deprivation has been linked to an increased risk of anxiety, depression, cardiovascular disease, and weight gain.
- The transition into sleep is not automatic. The body and mind need clear signals that it is time to move from alertness into rest.

Many people carry the energy and stress of the day straight into bed without a proper wind-down phase. As a result, their mind remains in problem-solving or "work" mode even while the body is trying to rest. This prevents full recovery and often leads to fragmented or shallow sleep. The good news is that we can increase the likelihood of experiencing greater quality sleep by doing two things: (1) helping the body get a head start on the detox process and (2) training our sleeping area to be the ultimate safety signal.

Before we focus on those two processes, let's establish your current baseline on the behaviors that most/all sleep books recommend in order to increase the potential for quality sleep.

Review the sleep optimization checklist that follows and check off what's already part of your daily sleep routine.

Sleep Optimization Checklist

MORNING

- Wake up at the same time every day (including weekends; limit "sleeping in" to $\leq$1 hour max)
- View natural outdoor sunlight within 30–60 minutes of waking (bright day: 10 minutes; cloudy: 20–30 minutes; overcast: up to 60 minutes)

- Get additional natural sunlight exposure in late afternoon/sunset (10–15 minutes)
- Outdoor UV-A exposure between 9 a.m. and 11 a.m. on eyes/skin to regenerate melatonin stores
- Delay caffeine intake for at least 90–120 minutes after waking (allows natural adenosine clearance)

DURING THE DAY

- Exercise regularly (3×/week), but finish at least 2–3 hours before bedtime (avoid late intense cardio)
- Limit caffeine after 12–2 p.m.
- Avoid or limit naps; if needed, keep <90 minutes and before ~3 p.m.
- Get daytime outdoor movement and light exposure whenever possible
- Avoid large/heavy meals within 3 hours of bedtime
- Take 5+ minute breaks from screens and cell phones during the day as often as possible

EVENING

- Dim all lights significantly after sunset; switch to warm/red-spectrum lighting only (candles, red bulbs, firelight). Avoid bright overhead lights after ~10 p.m.
- Wear blue-light blocker glasses (435–465 nm blocking) after sunset if using artificial light
- Take a hot bath or shower 1–2 hours before bed (decreases core body temperature)
- Establish a relaxing pre-bed routine (reading, journaling, lymphatic drainage, gratitude)
- Keep bedroom cool (64–67°F/15.5–19.5°C ideal)
- Keep bedroom dark and quiet (blackout curtains, earplugs/white noise if needed)
- Use bed for sleep and intimacy only—no work, screens, or stimulating activities
- Eliminate all light sources in bedroom (clocks, phone out of room or airplane mode far away; even tiny lights suppress melatonin)

- Minimize non-native EMFs at night (turn off wifi/router, unplug devices)
- Avoid alcohol, nicotine, and heavy meals 3–4+ hours before bed

Now that you have checked the behaviors that you currently engage in, review the checklist one additional time. Your task this round is to review all of the behaviors that are unchecked and choose one that you will begin to incorporate into your sleep routine starting tonight. Your focus is on training that additional sleep behavior until it becomes an automatic part of your sleep routine (i.e., a habit). Then review the sleep checklist again and choose another unchecked sleep behavior to train.

Critical Insight from the Classroom

From an evolutionary perspective, one of the greatest inventions in human history may also carry one of the greatest hidden costs: unnatural light.

For most of human history, when the sun went down, activity slowed. Darkness created a natural boundary. You couldn't extend productivity deep into the night. As light faded, so did stimulation. The body followed predictable circadian rhythms. Melatonin rose. Recovery began.

Then we invented light.

At first, it extended the evening modestly. Then came electricity. Then screens. Then the smartphone. Now, we live in a world that is effectively 24/7.

In global organizations, work never really stops. Someone, somewhere, is online. Emails arrive at all hours. Notifications don't respect time zones. And many of the participants we work with remain connected to technology right up until bedtime.

The pattern is strikingly consistent.

Laptop closed.

Phone set down.

Lights off.

Eyes shut.

And then. . . hope.

"I fall asleep pretty easily," we often hear. "But I wake up around 2 a.m. and then everything goes sideways."

Racing thoughts. Mental replay. Planning tomorrow's conversations. Revisiting unresolved issues. Reconnecting to daily stress in the middle of the night—when there is very little that can be done to solve any of it.

Two hours later, maybe sleep returns. Then the alarm goes off.

What's happening here is not mysterious.

When you stay cognitively and emotionally activated right up until the moment you try to sleep, your nervous system doesn't automatically downshift because the screen went dark. Blue light exposure suppresses melatonin production. Cognitive stimulation keeps the prefrontal cortex engaged. Emotional content—even subtle stress from emails or news—keeps the stress response humming quietly in the background.

So when you wake naturally in the early morning hours—which is normal—the system is primed for activation rather than restoration. The mind latches onto unfinished loops. Cortisol begins its natural early rise. And without proper wind-down, the brain shifts into problem-solving mode instead of drifting back into deep sleep.

What's most revealing is this: for many participants, the first time they think intentionally about sleep is when they get into bed.

They don't have a wind-down practice. They don't create separation from work. They simply hope for good sleep—often on the very nights they "need it more than ever."

But restorative sleep is not accidental. It is the outcome of deliberate preparation.

Just as you wouldn't expect elite performance without warm-up, you cannot expect deep recovery without wind-down.

(*continued*)

(continued)

That might mean setting a technology cutoff time. Dimming lights in the evening. Creating a simple ritual that signals to the brain, "Work is done. It is safe to power down." Light stretching. Gratitude journaling. Breathwork. Reading something calming instead of stimulating.

Sleep is your most powerful recovery tool. But in a 24/7 world, it requires intention.

Because while unnatural light extended our productivity, it also removed the natural cues that once protected our recovery.

And in today's environment, protecting sleep isn't passive.

It's strategic.

Setting Your Body for Quality Sleep

In our experience training thousands of people over the past three decades, we have learned that there are two simple and practical tools that help the body shift from an active state to a more restful one as you prepare for bed. These practices are designed to support both the quality and effectiveness of your sleep, allowing your system to do the deep work of detox, repair, and renewal overnight.

The two exercises you are about to learn are designed to support your body and mind in preparing for restful sleep. The goal is to associate these practices with your bed and bedtime routine. For best results, we highly recommend that you practice the two activities that follow literally as the last things you do before you physically get into bed. This pairing of the two activities with you physically getting into bed will train the association of your bed with detox and the safety signal.

The two simple strategies that help initiate your body's detoxification process and send it a clear message of safety are:

- A brief lymphatic drainage practice
- An effective and slightly unconventional gratitude practice

Let's begin with the physical practice that supports your body's natural detox: lymphatic drainage.

Understanding the Lymphatic System

The lymphatic system is one of the most overlooked yet essential systems in your body. It acts as a drainage and filtration network, working silently to remove waste, fight infection, and support your immune system.[6]

Imagine a web of tiny tubes running through your entire body. These are your lymph vessels. They carry a fluid called lymph, a clear, watery substance rich in white blood cells. Interestingly, your body contains nearly as much lymph as blood.

While blood distributes oxygen, nutrients, and hormones, lymph serves a different purpose:

- It helps drain away cellular waste
- It supports the immune system by transporting lymphocytes (a type of white blood cell)
- It assists in absorbing dietary fats into the bloodstream

A few key components of the lymphatic system include:

- **Lymph nodes:** Small bean-shaped filters that trap germs and waste
- **Lymph vessels:** Pathways that carry lymph through your body
- **Spleen:** Filters blood and removes old red blood cells
- **Thymus:** Produces immune cells during childhood

Why This Matters for Sleep and Recovery

The lymphatic system plays a critical role in detoxification. It removes waste, toxins, and excess fluid from tissues. When this system is sluggish or blocked, it can lead to a buildup of harmful substances and trigger stress signals in the body.[7]

Some of the consequences of a poorly functioning lymphatic system:

- Fatigue and a general sense of malaise
- Swelling and water retention
- Reduced ability to fight off infections
- Greater toxic load in the body
- Long-term risk of chronic conditions such as autoimmune disorders and digestive issues

Each of these signals tells your nervous system that something is wrong, keeping you in a stress response and disrupting sleep.[8]

The Big 6: A Two-Minute Lymphatic Drainage Routine

Fortunately, there is a simple two-minute routine you can do every night right before bed. It is known as the *Big 6 Lymph Reset* and was developed by Dr. Perry Nickelston to activate lymph flow and support your body's natural detoxification.

The practice involves targeted stimulation of six key areas where lymph tends to collect and become stagnant (Figure 13.1). By working with these areas, by rubbing, tapping, circling them you help your body begin its nightly detox and send it a message of calm and safety.

You can also follow along with a video demonstration by searching "Big 6 Lymph Reset" by Dr. Perry Nickeston.

Here is a quick overview of the six main areas to focus on. For each one, you will use your hand to gently rub, tap, and finally make slow circles on each side of the body:

1. Above and below the collarbone
2. Sides of the neck just below the ears
3. Upper chest and armpits
4. Abdomen
5. Hip crease
6. Behind the knees

Rubbing the area begins to loosen the lymph. Tapping and performing circles over the area gets the lymph moving.

This short ritual can become a powerful anchor in your evening routine, helping your system slow down, clear out the day and shift into a deeper state of rest.

The step-by-step process is as follows:

Area 1: Above and below the collarbone

- Use your entire hand, not just your fingers
- Rub above and below your collarbone (minimum of 20 times) Start with the left collarbone

- Tap the same area (minimum of 20 times)
- Rub in circles over the area (minimum of 20 times)
- Repeat the rub, tap, circle practice on the right collarbone

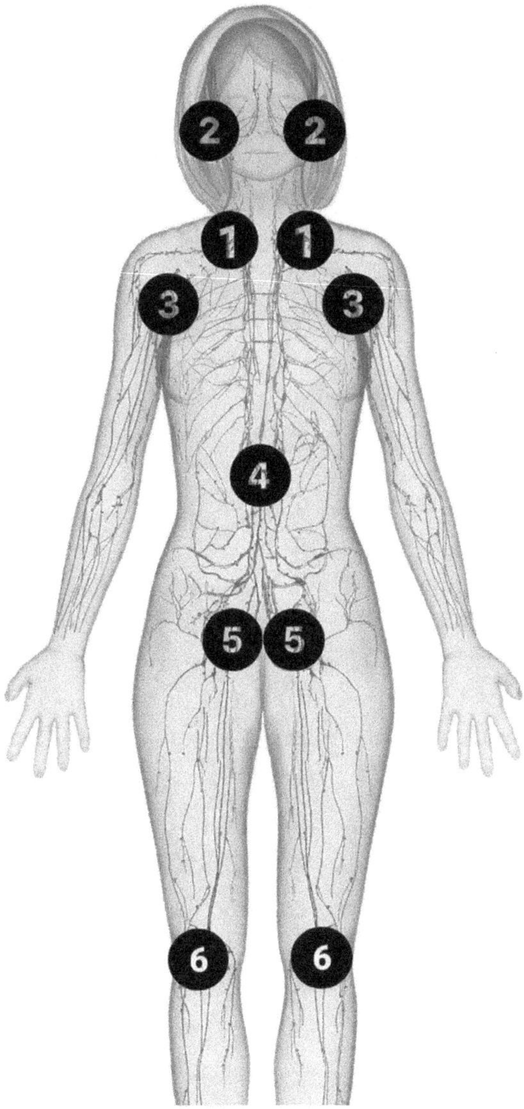

Figure 13.1 Big 6 Lymph Reset areas of focus.

Area 2: Below the ears (the "dip" in the area below your earlobe and your jawbone)

- Rub, tap, and circle (minimum of 20 times each) on the left side
- If tapping feels uncomfortable, simply rub for more repetitions
- Repeat on the right side

Area 3: Upper chest and armpits

- Place your hand on your left pectoral muscle, near the crease in your left armpit
- Rub, tap, and circle this area (minimum of 20 times each)
- Repeat on the right pectoral muscle

Area 4: Abdomen

- This a crucial area for drainage given the amount of sitting most people are doing daily, which compresses the lymph in the abdominal area
- Place one hand over your navel and the other hand above your navel
- Rub up and down over your abdomen with both hands (minimum of 20 times)
- Tap your abdomen with both hands (minimum of 20 times)
- Place one hand on top of the other hand and do counterclockwise circles on your abdomen (minimum of 20 times)

Area 5: Hip crease

- Place your hands on the interior of both sides of your hip bone (right hand on right side, left hand on left side)
- Using both hands at the same time: rub, tap, circle the area (minimum of 20 times each)

Area 6: Behind the knees

- Place each hand over the crease (bend) area behind each knee
- Using both hands at the same time: rub, tap, circle the area (minimum of 20 times each)

Once all six areas have been stimulated, stand up and gently bounce on your toes or shake your body for 15 to 20 seconds. This helps move lymph fluid and signals to your system that the detox process has begun. Again, we recommend you practice this activity as the last thing you do every night before physically getting into bed.

Gratitude as a Nighttime Practice

The second of the two simple strategies to help initiate your body's detoxification process and send it a clear message of safety is a simple gratitude practice. Gratitude is one of the most effective and underused tools we have to shift our internal states.[9] Practicing gratitude just before bed creates a powerful shift. As you begin to associate your bed and your evening routine with the feeling of appreciation, you're training your body to release its grip on tension and stress. You begin to pair sleep with safety. And that matters more than you may think.

Gratitude practice is often associated with journaling prompts such as "write down three to five things that you're grateful for today," "who is someone in your life that you are grateful for?" or "send a message of gratitude to someone in your life once per day."

You might have tried those classic gratitude exercises before, and perhaps you found them helpful. But for many people, the impact of listing what they're grateful for fades quickly or doesn't stick at all.

What we have experienced in following up with our training participants is that although everyone acknowledges the importance and effectiveness of experiencing gratitude, making a "list" mentally or literally everyday become what many describe as a "homework assignment" that very few people sustain.

That's because most approaches ask you to think your way into gratitude. Yet gratitude isn't a cognitive state. It's a feeling. And feelings live in the body.

Given our mission as a company is to provide you with strategies that are effective, practical, and most importantly, you will do, we needed to find a different gratitude practice that was simple and effective without becoming a "homework assignment."

When we feel gratitude, not just naming it or thinking about it, we begin to calm the nervous system in a very real, physiological way. Gratitude and stress cannot coexist in the body at the same time. So, if you're looking for something that can reliably signal to your system that it's safe to rest and detox, the gratitude practice that we are about to describe meets those criteria as it creates a deeper, more embodied experience.

How to Practice

The key is not to focus on what you're grateful for, but instead on a moment when someone expressed genuine gratitude toward you.[10] This is where the shift happens. Rather than searching for positive thoughts, you tap into a real emotional experience and your body responds accordingly.[11]

Here is the three step process.

Step 1:

Think of a specific moment when someone truly appreciated something you did; the person expressed gratitude TO YOU. Maybe you helped a friend through a hard time or went out of your way for a colleague. Perhaps a family member shared heartfelt thanks for your presence or support.

If nothing personal comes to mind right away, you can draw from a story that moved you, a moment of heartfelt appreciation in a book, a movie or something you heard in a conversation. The important thing is that it resonates with you emotionally. You're not just recalling a fact; you're stepping into the feeling.

Write down a brief headline of who expressed gratitude to you. We will get more detailed in a moment.

____

____

____

Step 2:
Try to bring the entire moment to mind, not just the words they said but the context. The more detail you can remember, the stronger the emotional impact. Let the scene come alive again. You may find your breath slowing, your shoulders dropping and your body softening as you reconnect with the memory.

Provide the following details:

What was the issue or challenge that the person was experiencing?

____

____

____

What did you do to help the person?

____

____

____

How did helping the person make you feel?

____

____

____

Step 3:
Once the "movie" is clear in your mind, devote a few minutes to closing your eyes or softening your gaze in order to step into the experience as if it is happening right now. Breathe into it. Feel the warmth of being appreciated. Let your body remember what that felt like.

Here is the magic of this practice; you don't need to find a new moment every night. In fact, repeating (training) the same story every night will deepen its impact over time. It becomes an anchor for your body to experience the safety signal. That means that simply recalling the experience will initiate the safety signal in your body. In addition, this practice doesn't need to be long, just one to three minutes is enough.

As this becomes part of your nightly rhythm, you're not only improving the quality of your sleep. You're building a habit of self-regulation. A way to guide yourself back into presence, calm, and inner steadiness. And that's a gift that will ripple through far more than just your experience sleeping.

By incorporating this gratitude experience practice into your nightly routine, you do far more than improve sleep quality—you literally retrain your nervous system to associate bedtime with safety, appreciation, and deep restoration. What begins as a simple two-minute ritual becomes a reliable bridge from the day's demands into genuine recovery, helping you wake with more energy and emotional bandwidth than you may have experienced in years. With your body now supported by both lymphatic drainage and this heart-centered practice, you are ready to address the next essential layer of your human energy system: your emotions.

In the following chapter we turn our attention to emotional regulation and, most importantly, to the critical distinction between stressors and stress itself—so you can stop reacting and start responding in ways that consistently move you toward your Best Self.

14

Managing Stressors

Before moving into feelings and emotions, let's begin by zooming in on what actually influences our emotions, specifically our stress reactions. In this chapter, we'll look at stressors.

We often view stress as people, things or even events in our lives. Those things are actually not stress. They are all stressors, which are external people or things that we have limited control or influence over. Stress is your response to those stressors.[1] This is a key delineation because we often devote a great deal of our focus on attempting to control, decrease, eliminate the stressors in our life, which drain our energy, when our focus needs to be on how we respond to those stressors.

This shift in focus is important because you most likely have little/no control over many of the stressors in your life, but you have complete control over your response or reaction to them; though it may not feel like you do at times. As such, it is your (effective or ineffective) response to stressors that determines the level of stress your experience. As the Stoic philosopher Epictetus said, "It's not what happens to you, but how you react to it that matters."

Imagine you step into the office on Monday morning and learn that your biggest client has decided to move their account to a competitor. That external event—the client's decision—is the stressor. It exists outside of you; you cannot control it in the moment. The stress, however, is what happens inside your body and mind once the news lands: the sudden spike in heart rate, the knot in your stomach, the racing thoughts about losing your bonus or looking incompetent in front of your boss. One colleague might feel the same news as a challenge to win the client back and experience only mild, motivating activation. Another might spiral into panic and self-doubt. The stressor is identical, yet the amount of stress each person feels is entirely determined by their internal response. This is why we can never eliminate every stressor, but we can dramatically reduce the stress we carry by learning to respond rather than react.

However you react to a stressor will determine your experience of stress. In the example above you might slip into internal reactions such as catastrophizing or adopting a victim mentality, or you can choose to pause, take a short walk outside, and digest the new information before responding. Learning to be intentional with our responses is essential, because automatic reactions, internal or external, often happen in the heat of the moment. Think back to the last time a colleague's email rubbed you the wrong way and you fired off a reply while your emotions were still running the show. The outcome probably created more stress and conflict than if you had taken a moment to gather yourself and responded once you felt calmer.

Stressors themselves are neither good nor bad. They affect everyone. What matters is unraveling and understanding your own response to the stressors in your life. As we have stated, the issue for most people is that they never learned how to respond to stressors effectively, which often leads to reacting (emotionally) rather than responding (logically).

Figure 14.1 depicts the typical stress response. A stressor occurs. You do not have a strategy or plan to effectively respond to it. . .so you react emotionally, which often leads to a less than optimal outcome (e.g., you behave negatively, you "act" calm when you are frustrated, etc.).

This response is a learned pattern shaped by the stressors you have encountered throughout your life. No two people react in exactly the same way. Your response at any moment depends on factors such as your mood, who you are with, the time of day, or even how recently you ate. Increasing your awareness of these patterns and the conditions that influence them allows you to choose different, more resourceful responses.

The question is, what response do you choose?

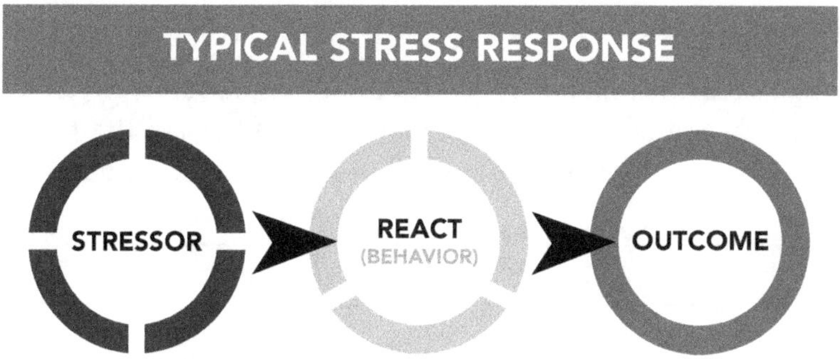

Figure 14.1 The typical stress response.

Strategies to Manage Chronic and Acute Stressors

To help you manage your response to stressors more effectively we first need to distinguish between the two general types of stressors you experience: chronic and acute.[2] At IHP we refer to chronic stressors as "always on" stressors and acute stressors as "in the moment" stressors.

Chronic stressors persist over a long period and rarely disappear fully. These are the pressures you know are coming, tasks or events you often dread, and some of them may even appear directly in your calendar. Examples include ongoing financial pressure, a high-demand job with no clear boundaries, a calendar filled with meetings every day, or caring for a chronically ill family member. Because these stressors often lack certainty and (known) conclusion (the two things our brain wants in every situation), the body remains in a heightened state of high energy. Over time this constant activation can impair your sleep and leave you feeling exhausted, anxious, or burned out, and wear down your physical health.

Acute stressors come on suddenly. Examples include a conflictual conversation, narrowly avoiding a car accident, giving an unexpected presentation, or receiving an urgent email. These stressors activate a burst of energy in the form of the danger signal (i.e., stress response) because the brain's instant reaction to something unexpected is to protect the organism (you) until it can determine what is going on (certainty) and how long it is going to last (conclusion).

The good news is that there are effective strategies to manage both the chronic and acute stressors that you experience in your life.

Chronic Stressors

The first step in responding to chronic stressors more effectively is becoming aware of what those stressors are. What are the top three chronic (ongoing) stressors that you have faced in recent months?

____

____

____

Next step, which chronic stressor has had the biggest negative impact on you being your Best Self?

____

Congratulations if you were able to identify your main chronic stressor, especially the one that has the biggest negative impact on you. This is the first step to developing a plan for handling this chronic stressor more effectively.

Managing Chronic Stressors: VIP

We often experience chronic stressors in broad terms, as if it were a single thing: "I'm stressed because of work," or "My children stress me out." This approach presents a challenge to our brain because, for all its great capabilities, our brain is very literal.

We're going to explain what we mean by "our brain is very literal" in a moment. Before we do, as we explain that statement. . .

Do not think of a white bear

Do not imagine the color red

Do not remember the sun

What happened as you read those commands?

You thought of a white bear.

You imagined the color red.

You remembered the sun.

Your brain is very literal. So, when you experience "work" as a chronic stressor, your brain literally experiences every component or variable involved in work as a stressor. There are potentially dozens or more components of "work" that become stressors.

Using our example of "work" your first step is to think through the various components involved in "work." For example: coworkers, physical setting, a demanding boss, the commute, endless last-minute deadlines, your workspace, deliverables, the lights, meeting times, smells, furniture, etc.

Getting specific about the components that make up your stressor gives you something more concrete to address.[3] You have little/no control or influence over the abstract stressor of "work," but you may believe that you can control/influence "your workspace," for example.

Once you list some of the components of the abstract stressor (e.g., work), you can then develop a proactive plan to manage it.

Re-write the chronic stressor that you feel has had the biggest negative impact on your being your Best Self more often.

____

Now, write down at least five components of that chronic stressor.

____

____

____

____

____

This initial step will, in of itself, begin to decrease your level of stress.

Next, pick one of the components you listed that you feel you have at some control and/or influence over.

____

Now we are going to apply the VIP model (Figure 14.2) to that component. This model addresses the three key aspects (Volume, Intensity, Perception) of chronic stressors that you can adjust to enable you to respond more effectively.

Figure 14.2 Break down a chronic stressor into its volume, intensity and (your) perception of it.

Adjusting even one of these components can create positive ripple effects across the others, helping you build greater resilience and improve your overall well-being.

Let's take a moment to explain each aspect of VIP:

- V = Volume = the size or amount of the stressor(s)
- I = Intensity = how strongly those stressor(s) impact you
- P = Perception = how you interpret or make meaning of those stressor(s)

VIP emerged from research on locus of control, which explores whether people feel that they have influence over their experiences or believe that outside forces determine what happens to them.[4] People with an external locus of control often attribute their feelings and outcomes to something outside of themselves, such as a boss, colleague, partner, or family member. With this perspective, they give away their ability to shape how they experience life, especially when it comes to stress.

Those with an internal locus of control, on the other hand, believe that their feelings and actions are influenced by their own choices and behaviors. This belief creates a sense of empowerment and ownership over how they respond to challenges and stressors.[5]

The VIP model is designed to help you strengthen your internal locus of control when it comes to chronic and ongoing stress. Rather than seeing stress as something that is either fully present or completely gone, VIP encourages you to view it as something that can be adjusted.

Each element, Volume, Intensity, and Perception, can be fine-tuned, like turning a dial. We use a dial analogy very purposefully because most people view stressors like a light switch; either they are "on" or they are "off." In reality, stressors are like dials; at times they are lower (2 out of 10) and at other times they are higher (8 out 10) on the dial.

Let's now explore the different ways you can adjust the three VIP dials on to better manage your experience of your chronic stressors.

Applying VIP

The next step in this process is to apply the VIP model to the component you wrote down previously. Remember, this is a process that you can apply to any chronic stressor in your life.

It's worth explaining that participants sometimes have a hard time distinguishing between Volume and Intensity because they are so closely related. Volume refers to "how much" and/or "how often" you are currently experiencing the component of the chronic stressor. Intensity describes the urgency you place (or others place) onto the component of the chronic stressor, which can spike when several urgent demands collide.

Now we are going to brainstorm ways to adjust the Volume, Intensity, and Perception of the component.

The goal of this process is not to simply provide readymade solutions but to help you ask better questions for each dial. When you plan proactively, you strengthen your ability to manage chronic, always-on stressors.

Now let's come back to the component of the chronic stressor that you identified for earlier and explore how you can use the VIP model for your own situation.

Using the component of your chronic stressor, begin to brainstorm answers to the following questions:

What are some things that you can do to control the volume of this stressor?

____

____

____

What are some things that you can do to control the intensity (urgency) with which you experience this stressor?

____

____

____

What are some things that you can do to control the perception you have of this stressor?

____

____

____

Critical Insight from the Classroom

In a recent session, we asked participants to identify their number one chronic stressor.

One participant said, without hesitation, "My health."

That's a heavy statement.

When we hear something that broad, we don't rush to solutions. Instead, we step into a coaching mindset and ask the simplest—and often most powerful—follow-up question:

"Tell me more."

It's almost impossible to address a stressor effectively when it's defined in such general terms. "My health" could mean sleep, weight, blood pressure, energy levels, chronic pain, or something else entirely. Without clarity, the stressor feels large, vague, and overwhelming.

As he unpacked it, the story became much more specific.

"Before COVID, I was in the office every day," he said. "That meant a lot of walking during my commute. Then moving between meetings in the building. And we had a great little gym—I'd work out two or three times a week for 45 minutes."

Then came the shift.

"Since we went fully remote, I'm basically at my desk all day. I move from my office to the kitchen to the living room. It's all very sedentary. I'm worried I'm not moving at all."

Now we had something concrete.

The stressor wasn't "my health." It was reduced movement due to a change in work environment.

That distinction matters.

When we asked what small, realistic adjustments he could make within the reality of a busy remote job, he paused and said, "I do like getting fresh air. Maybe I could be more disciplined about going outside between meetings."

"Perfect," we said.

Then came the key question: "If you do that consistently, how will the intensity of this stressor change?"

He smiled.

"Well, I've now got a different story in my head. What I'm really worried about is lack of movement—and now I'm addressing it in a way that actually fits my life."

In that moment, you could see the shift across all three dials of the VIP model.

First, the **Volume** of the stressor decreased. "My health" became "I'm moving less than I used to."

Second, the **Intensity** lowered because he was taking action. A sense of control returned.

Third, his **Perception** changed. The narrative moved from broad and overwhelming to specific and manageable.

The power of "Tell me more" is that it breaks apart the fog.

When you assume the role of coach—even with yourself—you create space between you and the stressor. You get curious. You clarify. And often, what felt enormous begins to feel actionable.

Sometimes the most transformative shift doesn't come from a dramatic overhaul.

It comes from narrowing the lens, adjusting the story, and turning one realistic dial at a time.

Note that all the strategies you just identified came from you. This is the power of self-awareness and reflection. You already hold much of the insight you need to reduce the impact of chronic, always-on stressors. While it's not always easy to implement these ideas in real life, and not every strategy will work in every situation, the point is to just begin. Start putting even small adjustments into practice.

What you have just done is called proactive planning. Unlike reactive planning, where we respond after stress hits, proactive planning allows you to anticipate stress and prepare for it in advance.[6] The VIP model is one way to do that. It is a practical process to help you break a stressor down, assess what you can influence and begin shifting how you experience it.

Now that we have explored how to take control of chronic or predictable stress, let us turn our attention to a different kind of challenge. Sudden and unexpected stressors can knock us off course in a moment. These acute stressors require a different kind of toolset, one that helps us ground ourselves and recover quickly, so that we are decreasing the likelihood of reacting emotionally.

Manage Acute Stressors with the Resilient Stress Response

Following our work on managing chronic stress, the Resilient Stress Response offers a practical strategy for acute unexpected or in the moment stressors. This approach is designed for those times when something urgent or unfamiliar happens, such as receiving an unexpected email at work, navigating a tense conversation, or stepping into a responsibility you do not face regularly, like giving a large presentation.

A key part of this response is labeling your emotions tied to the experience before reacting.[7] For example, during or after a conflictual conversation you might notice and say, "I am feeling frustrated," rather than making judgments about someone else's behavior. This is a key point, you label the experience, not the person. Saying the person is "frustrating," while potentially true in the moment, is training your brain to identify that person with the feeling of frustration.

Science supports this simple emotional labeling strategy. Researchers at UCLA used brain imaging to study how people respond to strong emotional stimuli such as images of angry or fearful faces. When participants passively viewed these images, their amygdala, the brain's emotional center, showed increased activity. But when they labeled the emotions by putting a word to what they saw on the pictures of people's faces, activity shifted from the amygdala to the prefrontal cortex, the area responsible for rational and logical thinking.[8]

This shift means that naming your emotions moves your brain from a reactive emotional state to a more thoughtful, logical one. That means that you shift from reacting emotionally to responding more logically.[9] The exact word you use is less important than the act of labeling itself. Whether you call the feeling frightening or frustrating, you are identifying the emotion tied to the experience. By practicing this labeling step, you create space to respond more productively rather than react impulsively.

For example, imagine you have two back-to-back meetings. In the first, you receive unexpected and challenging feedback. You need to move quickly to the next meeting, but your mind is still caught up in what just happened. If you don't take a moment to process, your mind keeps replaying that first meeting. You enter the second meeting distracted and emotionally reactive, carrying frustration or stress from earlier. This makes it hard to focus and engage fully, and your performance suffers.

Now, imagine a different approach. Before stepping into the next meeting, you pause and name how you feel about the previous experience. You might say to yourself, "That last meeting was frustrating." This simple act of labeling your emotion helps to decrease the activity in the emotional area of your brain, increase the activity in the logic area to be more present for your next interaction.

This shift means naming your emotions moves your brain from a reactive, emotional state to a more thoughtful, responsive, logical one (Figure 14.3). The exact word you use is less important than the act of labeling itself. Whether you call the feeling frightening or frustrating, you are identifying the emotion tied to the experience and not defining the other person. By using this resilient stress response tool, you create space to respond more productively instead of reacting impulsively.

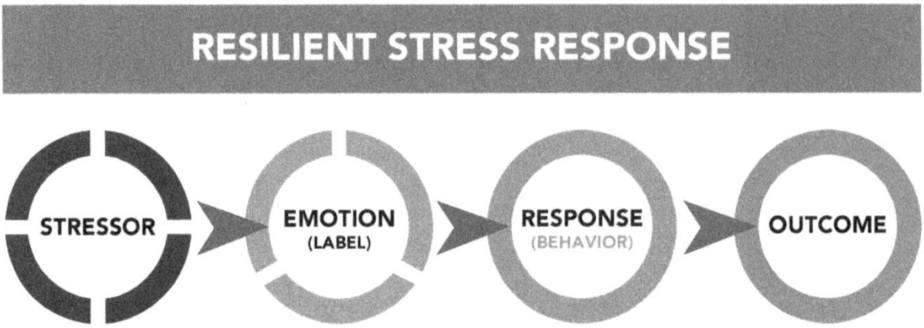

Figure 14.3 Using an emotional label to respond to a stressor rather than reacting to it.

The Resilient Stress Response can be understood as a sequence of four important steps shown in the graphic above. First, you encounter a stressor, which could be anything unexpected or challenging, like a difficult conversation or an urgent email. The next step is to identify and label the emotion that arises from this experience. This means putting a name to what you are feeling such as frustration, anxiety, or confusion. Labeling the emotion helps shift your brain from an emotional reaction toward a more thoughtful state.[10] The third step is your response, which is the behavior or action you take after naming your emotion. Because you have created mental space, your response becomes more intentional and constructive. Finally, this leads to a more positive or effective outcome where your actions produce better results, and you feel more in control. Together, these steps form a powerful tool to manage stress with clarity and presence.

To summarize, emotional labeling is about hitting pause and putting words to how you're feeling right there in the moment. By pausing and labeling the emotion, a few things happen in your brain. The act of finding a word interrupts your emotional reaction and activates your logical brain, where the exact words or perceived emotions don't really matter.

It gives your brain two things it craves: certainty about what's happening and a sense of conclusion about how long it will last.

You're letting your brain know what this is, an emotional experience, and that it's now over. That message allows your body to calm down and be open to connection again. Without it, the brain keeps replaying the scene and training your nervous system to react to it over and over. And remember, whatever you repeat, whether a thought, feeling or behavior, you're reinforcing it.

Labeling your emotions doesn't mean you forget what happened. You'll still remember that challenging meeting, but you won't be emotionally charged about it anymore. When it comes to mind, it will feel more like a neutral memory than an activated moment.

Ideally, you'd label the emotion as close to the experience as possible, as this reduces how much your brain and body encode the stress response as a lasting pattern. You can still reduce the emotional charge even later on. It just may take more repetition because that emotional movie has been playing for longer. This tool is not for deep trauma, but for everyday disruptions, friction, and frustrations.

If you've ever named your toddler's feelings mid meltdown by saying something like, "You seem frustrated" to help them calm down, you've already seen this in action. And just as it works for children, it also works for us.

Let's now look at how these acute, unexpected stressors show up in your day and when you may have had a response you weren't proud of.

Describe an experience where you responded poorly to an unexpected stressor.

____

____

____

What were the consequences of reacting in this way?

____

____

____

What emotional label could you have used to describe the stressor?

____

____

Reflecting on the story you just wrote down, notice how naming the emotion can already change how you relate to it. Even though the moment has passed, the emotional impact often lingers in the body and nervous system. Emotional labeling is a simple yet powerful way to bring awareness to what you're feeling and can help you start shifting how your brain and body store the experience. One client summed up this strategy well with a simple phrase that stuck across their entire organization. "Name it to tame it." That reminder alone helped people stay present, reduce reactivity, and build trust in their response.

Critical Insight from the Classroom

In one session, a participant shared something that initially seemed contradictory.

"A big part of my job is presenting to large groups," she said. "And I love it. It's my favorite part of the role."

Then she paused.

"But right when I step onto the stage, I can feel myself getting flustered. My heart spikes. My thoughts scatter. For a few seconds, I'm not fully there."

That moment—the exact moment she needed clarity most—was where her physiology was working against her.

This is where the Resilient Stress Response becomes so powerful.

We often associate stress with negative situations—conflict, deadlines, uncertainty. But from a biological perspective, stress is simply the body's mobilization of energy in response to perceived demand. The body doesn't categorize experiences as "good" or "bad." It categorizes them as activating.

Public speaking is a perfect example.

Even if you love it, stepping in front of a large group is socially evaluative. Your nervous system recognizes that you are being observed. It mobilizes energy. Heart rate increases. Adrenaline rises. Attention sharpens.

That activation isn't inherently negative.

The challenge is interpretation.

If that surge is labeled internally as "I'm nervous," "I'm losing control," or "I hope I don't mess this up," the stress response can tip toward reactivity. Blood flow prioritizes survival circuits. Thoughts narrow. You feel flustered.

But if that same physiological surge is labeled differently, something remarkable happens.

Research in emotional labeling and cognitive reappraisal shows that simply naming an emotion—especially in a way that reframes activation as readiness—can regulate the amygdala and support prefrontal function. In other words, the act of labeling changes the body's response.

We explained to her that emotional labeling works in both negative and positive high-stress moments. The difference is the label.

Next time you step onto the stage, as we suggested, take one slow breath and internally acknowledge what you're feeling:

"I'm excited."
"I'm ready."
"I'm prepared."
"This energy is helping me."
That's it.

That subtle shift activates what we call the Resilient Stress Response—a state where activation is harnessed rather than suppressed. Blood flow remains available to the brain's executive centers. Emotional regulation stabilizes. Physiology settles just enough to keep you sharp without tipping into overwhelm.

When she tried it, she later reported something simple but profound: "The energy didn't disappear. It just felt useful."

That's the superpower.

You don't need to eliminate activation. In many performance moments, you don't want to. You need to interpret it skillfully.

The resilient stress response isn't about being calm all the time. It's about channeling activation with awareness.

Even in moments you love, your body may still mobilize. The difference between flustered and focused can come down to a single breath—and the story you attach to the sensation.

Now that we've explored how to respond more effectively to both chronic and acute stressors, let's turn our attention to what may actually the most significant source of stress in our lives; our thoughts. Specifically, the often unspoken stories that we tell ourselves about the choices we make, the experiences we have, and the circumstances in our lives.

15

Narrating Your Way to Your Best

We have now arrived at the final component of the human energy system: your thoughts (Figure 15.1). Just as your emotions and behaviors influence your energy, your thoughts shape how you interpret and respond to the world around you. In this chapter, we explore one of the most powerful drivers of the human experience: the stories you tell yourself.

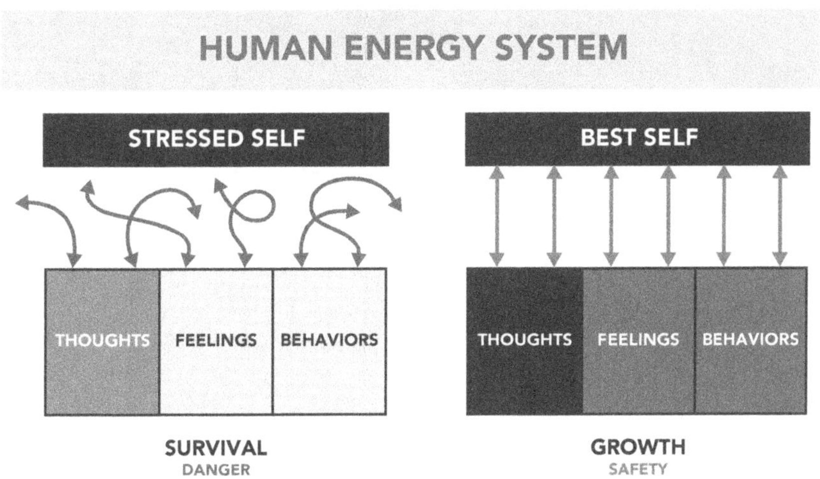

Figure 15.1 The human energy system.

The thoughts you repeat become the internal narratives that shape your perception of yourself, of others and of life. Over time, these stories form beliefs. And beliefs, once repeated and reinforced, become part of your identity.[1] You will always behave in ways that match the identity you hold, whether that identity empowers you or holds you back.

Think about how many stories are running in your mind on a typical day. Some are subtle and automatic. Others are loud and persistent. "I never have time." "I am not good with money." "People always let me down." Or on the flip side: "I find a way through." "I am strong when it counts." The question is not whether you are telling stories. It is whether you are aware of them and how they are shaping your life.

The stories we tell ourselves are not just fleeting thoughts. From a neuroscience perspective, every repeated thought strengthens a connection between two parts of the brain called synapses.[2] The more often we think a certain way, the stronger and more automatic that pathway becomes. This is how stories turn into beliefs.

Figure 15.2 illustrates how an initial story can become part of who we are. For example, if you are someone who currently does not get much movement in your day and you want to start to exercise. So, you

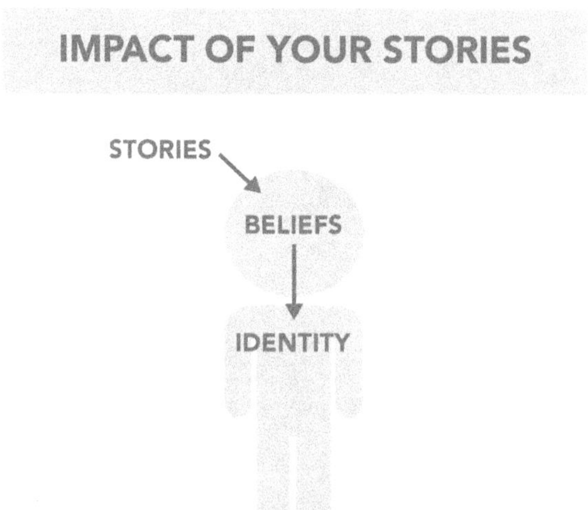

Figure 15.2 When you train a story enough times it becomes a belief. As you continue to train that belief over time it becomes part of your identity.

tell yourself a "new" alternative story that you are going to start exercising. Each time you behave in alignment with that thought (i.e., you exercise) and experience a shift in how you are feeling as a result of your behavior (i.e., exercising), the story becomes more deeply wired into your brain; as we have stated repeatedly throughout this book, any thought, feeling, or behavior you repeat. . .you are training.

Over time and repetition, this story shifts from being just a thought and becomes a belief. The potential challenge here is that we human beings hold our beliefs to be true—whether they are or not in reality is a different story. And the more you train that belief, the more it becomes a part of your identity—and you will always behave in line with your identity. This is true for helpful beliefs as well as limiting ones. That's why the thoughts and stories you repeat matter so much. They literally shape who you are.

Up until this point, you have started to build a better understanding of who you are at your best. You defined your three Best Self words. You began noticing which of those qualities tends to disappear first under stress or pressure. You also identified the kinds of situations in which you show up aligned with your best, as well as those where you do not.

This process gave you a strong intellectual foundation. You are becoming more aware of the difference between when you are showing up as your best and when you are not. But now it is time to go deeper.

Awareness is only the beginning. The next step is to train your mind to be that version of yourself more often. Every thought, feeling, and behavior that you repeat becomes part of your personal reality and eventually your identity.[3] Given that you are constantly telling yourself stories, experiencing feelings related to those stories and usually behaving in line with those stories, you are always training something. So, the question becomes: What do you choose to train?

One of the most effective tools we have is mental rehearsal. This is the practice of imagining a specific scenario and seeing yourself move through it in alignment with your Best Self. It's like creating a mental movie in your head.[4] The more you play the movie, the more natural it becomes for your brain to act that way in real life.

In this case, the movie you are creating is of you showing up as your Best Self. You are visualizing what that version of you looks like, sounds like, and feels like. This builds a neural blueprint. And because the brain does not distinguish between what is vividly imagined and what is real, this practice becomes a powerful way to create new pathways, patterns, and eventually, identity.

Over time, mental rehearsal helps you shift from an idea of your Best Self into the experience of being it. You don't just think about who you want to be. You start becoming that person, one thought at a time. The stories you tell yourself eventually become beliefs. With enough repetition, those beliefs shape your identity. And your identity determines how you act and respond to life. As we've stated, you will always behave aligned with your identity.

Keep in mind, you do not have just one identity. You have a different identity for each area of your life: work, family, health, finances, and more. Each of these identities began with a story. Many of those stories were shaped by forces outside of you. They were influenced by family, culture, media, school, and past experiences. Some of these stories are empowering. Others are outdated or limiting but are still playing quietly in the background.

A Study on the Power of Thought

As we've explored, the stories we tell ourselves hold remarkable power. They don't just influence our thoughts and emotions. They shape how we feel physically and how we show up in the world. To illustrate just how impactful our internal narratives are, consider this: Researchers have found that when people consciously changed their internal narratives about a stressful event, they experienced lower stress levels, improved coping, and greater overall well-being. This isn't just about thinking positively. It's about rewiring how your brain responds to challenges. What you tell yourself in those moments can either escalate your stress or help you move through it with clarity. The stories you choose to believe are not just words. They become the lens through which you see your reality.

A compelling example of this comes from a Harvard University study led by psychologist Alia Crum. The research explored how our beliefs about our daily activities can actually influence physical health, even when the activities themselves remained unchanged.[5]

In the study, 84 female hotel room attendants were divided into two groups. One group was told that the physical activity involved in cleaning hotel rooms counted as effective exercise and met the Surgeon General's recommendations for an active lifestyle. They were also given examples to help reframe their work as physical fitness. The second group was told nothing at all.

After just four weeks with no changes to their actual workload or routine, the group that received this information began to perceive their work differently. They reported feeling more active and, even more strikingly, showed significant improvements in several health markers including weight, blood pressure, body fat, waist-to-hip ratio, and BMI. The control group, by contrast, showed no such changes.

Same work. Different story. Radically different outcomes.

This study makes clear that when you shift your perspective, you can shift your physiology. Your thoughts create a kind of blueprint for how your body reacts, copes, and heals. Just like those hotel maids, you can train your mind to support rather than sabotage you.

Now let's look more closely at how those stories get built and what you can do to shift the ones that are holding you back. Remember that you may be telling yourself different stories in different areas of your life. Since the stories mainly determine how you act and feel, it's crucial to first become aware of them in order to change them. Everything you say or think is your story.

Critical Insight from the Classroom

We were working through the sleep section when a participant casually said something that made the room pause.

"I don't sleep."

That's a bold statement.

"Tell us more about that," we said.

"I've always had problems sleeping," he replied. "As I've gotten older, I've just had to come to terms with the fact that I don't sleep."

(*continued*)

(*continued*)

There it was. Not a complaint. Not frustration. A conclusion. A story.

We began exploring some of the foundational factors around sleep hygiene—technology use before bed, lighting, temperature, alcohol, meal timing. He listened patiently.

"Tried all of that," he said. "Nothing works for me."

We shifted to caffeine.

"I used to drink a lot of coffee," he admitted. "But I cut way back. Now it's just one espresso first thing in the morning. So it's not the coffee."

"Have you ever tried giving it up completely?" we asked.

"It's not the coffee," he repeated. "I hardly drink any now."

And here lies the power of story—for good or for bad.

When a story becomes entrenched—*I don't sleep*—it closes doors. It filters evidence. It narrows experimentation. It becomes identity, not hypothesis.

We gently pushed one last time.

"Humor us. Cut out that early morning espresso for a couple of weeks and just see what happens."

"I'll give it a try," he said—not convinced, but willing.

About a month later, we received an email.

"I had my first unbroken six hours of sleep in 20 years."

Twenty years.

He went on to explain that he later discovered he metabolizes caffeine about four times slower than the average person. That early morning espresso? For his physiology, it was the equivalent of drinking coffee late in the evening.

We were amazed.

But the deeper insight wasn't about caffeine.

It was about narrative.

Our stories shape our behavior far more than we realize. When a belief becomes fixed—*this is just how I am*—we stop experimenting. We stop questioning. We stop looking for levers we may have missed.

The story had become self-sealing.

Sleep deprivation wasn't just a problem he was trying to solve. It had become part of his identity.

And identity-level stories are powerful. They conserve energy—the brain likes certainty—but they can also quietly trap us in patterns that undermine our well-being.

The lesson here isn't that caffeine is always the culprit.

It's that curiosity must stay alive.

Instead of "I don't sleep," the more productive story becomes, "I haven't found the right lever yet."

That small shift keeps doors open.

In stress, performance, and recovery, we see this again and again. The stories we carry about ourselves—our resilience, our limitations, our habits—can either create possibility or quietly shut it down.

Sometimes the breakthrough isn't in a new strategy.

It's in being willing to challenge the story you've been telling yourself for years.

The Stories You Tell Yourself

It's important to be very honest with yourself when you start reflecting on the stories you tell yourself. This honesty matters when it comes to seeing, challenging, and especially changing the stories that are somehow holding you back. Some stories are rooted in truth, but many are filled with assumptions. Some stories you tell yourself you may even like, which means you might be unconsciously holding on to them.

The way to shift your identity over time is to become conscious of the story you are telling and begin to change it. This process requires you to change your perspective and get out of your current routine because it simply reminds you of who you think you are. When you create space to reflect, you can see the story for what it is, not a fact, but a pattern. And once you see it, you can begin to tell a new one.[6,7]

Your thoughts happen fast, sometimes too fast to catch and challenge in the moment. That's why stepping out of your usual routine and environment is crucial. When you change your physical or mental space, you create the distance needed to see your story with fresh eyes.

Think about this:

If you are dealing with a stressful situation at work, trying to examine your story more objectively while still in the story's environment (i.e., work) is very challenging. Your mind is too caught up in the moment, the emotions are high, and your usual patterns are in play. Instead, what if you took a step back, maybe went for a walk outside, took a quiet moment alone or journaled later at home?

In this new space, ask yourself the following questions:

- What story had I told myself about a stressor in my life?
- What were the consequences in my life if I had chosen to continue to train that story?
- Who am I without that story?
- What alternative, more helpful story am I telling myself about that stressor?

Before you answer each question, notice the way that the questions are written. The first two questions are in the past tense (i.e., had I told myself. . .), whereas the other two questions are written in the present tense. Your task here is to answer the first question, "What story had I told myself about a stressor in my life?" talking about yourself in the past tense and in the third person. For example, if your name is Kevin, you would start your answer to the first question something like, "In the past Kevin believed that he could never write a book on managing stress more effectively."

This may seem like a very odd directive, but here is what is going on in your mind when you answer the question this way—it starts to believe that the story is in the past and no longer occurring now, even if it is a story that you have currently been telling yourself.

As awkward as it may feel when you answer the question this way, it is the first step in diminishing the negative impact of that story because your brain starts to believe that it is in the past.

Answer the second question, "What were the consequences in my life if I had chosen to continue training that story? in the past conditional tense (e.g., the consequences would have been. . .). Answering the question this way safely provides your brain with an idea of what the consequences (i.e., in your life) might have been. For better or worse, what gets most human beings to truly begin to change is examination, or actual experience, of the consequences (i.e., pain) of continuing on the same path.

Answer the third question, "Who am I without that story?" in the present tense. This question begins to make you aware of your identity associated with the story in the first question. As we discussed earlier in this section, when a story gets repeated enough times, over time, it eventually becomes a part of our identity. This question begins the process of you developing an identity that does not include the problematic story. For example, if Kevin's story has always been that he was not qualified or knowledgeable enough to write a book, his answer to this question might be something like, "Without the story that I'm not qualified or knowledgeable enough to write a book, I am a capable and creative individual with unique experiences and insights to share. I am confident in my ability to learn, grow, and express my ideas through writing. I am someone who can inspire and connect with others through the stories I tell."

Also answer the fourth question, "What alternative, more helpful story am I telling myself about that stressor?" in the first person, present tense (e.g., I am. . .). In doing so, understand that it may seem awkward to talk about an alternative story as if you have already been telling yourself that story. By answering the question this way, you are telling your mind that you are already thinking this way and by using "I am. . ." you are developing a new identity associated with this more helpful story. Continuing the Kevin book writing example, your answer to this question might be something like, "My unique experiences and perspectives are valuable and worth sharing through writing. I trust that my knowledge is enough to create a meaningful book, and I can continue to learn and refine my craft along the way. This story empowers me to embrace my creativity and take bold steps toward authorship."

This is the beginning of you retraining a different, more helpful story about a specific stressor.

Devote time now to answer all four questions and note how you feel as you answer each one.

What story have I told myself about a stressor in my life? (Answer in the past tense, using the third person.)

What were the consequences in my life if I had chosen to continue training that story? (Answer using phrasing "my life would have. . .")

Who am I without this story? (Answer in the present tense.)

What alternative, more helpful, story am I telling myself about the stressor? (Answer in the present tense.)

This distance allows for greater objectivity and creativity. It opens up room for new perspectives that weren't visible when you were "in" the story.

Shifting Your Perspective, Changing Your Story

By removing yourself from the setting and stepping back, you gain the distance necessary to look at your story with greater objectivity. This shift allows you to spot assumptions, patterns, and beliefs you might otherwise miss. It's a way to pause the fast-moving thoughts and give yourself the chance to consider alternative narratives. Changing your story is not an instant fix; it's a process that requires awareness, patience, and practice. But when you make this shift, the payoff is profound: a life in which stress no longer controls you and where you can choose empowering stories that serve your well-being and growth.

Moving Forward: Rewriting the Narrative

The Harvard Maid Study, along with broader research on mindset, underscores one of the central messages of this chapter: Your story significantly impacts your quality of life. The words you repeat internally about your work, your relationships or your challenges are not background noise. They shape your brain, your health, and your future.

Your ability to rewrite your story does not come from ignoring challenges. It comes from meeting them with clarity, compassion, and a willingness to choose a different narrative, one that supports your well-being and your growth.

What you tell yourself regularly shapes your entire reality. Are you telling yourself "I'm failing, I am stuck, I can't?" Or are you telling yourself "I'm growing, I'm evolving, I can?"

Remember, you choose the story that you want to train. The question is which story about yourself will you train?

You now possess the complete internal map: a clear picture of your Stressed Self and Best Self, the science of how stress and recovery operate in your body and brain, and the powerful practice of rewriting the stories that shape your identity. Awareness and strategies alone, however, remain theoretical until they are lived. That is why we move now from insight to implementation. In Part 3 you will translate everything you have learned into a practical, personalized action system designed for real life—the life that still contains back-to-back meetings, family obligations, and unexpected curveballs. You will build a Recovery Menu that fits your actual schedule, commit to a single Micro Mission that creates momentum, and intentionally shape your environment so your Best Self becomes the easier, more automatic choice. The journey of transformation is no longer "someday." It begins today, one intentional action at a time.

PART III
Action

"Every action you take is a vote for the type of person you wish to become."

—James Clear

16

Planning Intentional Recovery

As YOU'VE LEARNED, intentional recovery is a thoughtful pause from work that helps recharge your human energy battery. It's important to remember that periods of stress or high energy need to be followed by periods of recovery or low energy expenditure. Recovery allows you to recharge your energy, which in turn helps you regulate your emotions, mental state, and behaviors more effectively in any situation. Again, the goal is not to recharge your battery back to 100% all at once, but to gain back incremental charges throughout the day a little here, a little there.

Just knowing that intentional recovery is important doesn't automatically mean you'll take more micro-breaks. One of the primary reasons people do not engage in intentional recovery during their business workday is because, in the midst of all the tasks, stimulation, distractions, they forget.[1] For example, if you have just a minute between meetings, by the time you think about taking a break, that minute may already be gone.

What will significantly increase the likelihood of you remembering to choose to intentionally recover during your workday is to develop a plan that is personal to you. . .and you will actually do. The key is to find short, manageable recovery moments that fit naturally into your day. As we've discussed, these little micro-breaks add up and help keep your energy and focus strong.

Generating Micro-Recovery Ideas

A helpful way to build your recovery plan is to think about what you can do in different amounts of time, whether you have one minute, five minutes or fifteen minutes (Figure 16.1). Your task is to come up with as many different intentional recovery options as you can, that are personal to you and you will do, for each time frame. The more options you have, the easier it will be to use whatever time you find during your day to reset and recharge.

Here are some examples:

One-Minute Recovery Ideas:

- Take three deep, slow breaths with a slightly longer exhale
- Calf raises
- Look outside

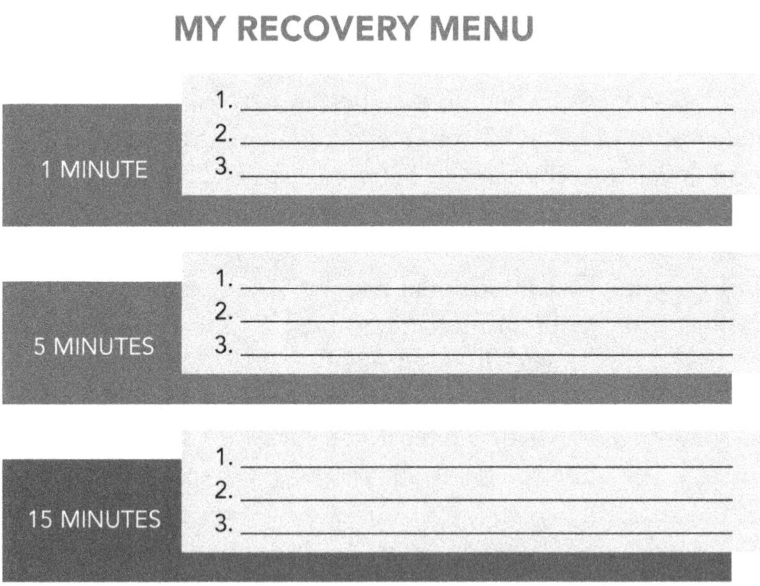

Figure 16.1 **Your personal recovery menu.**

- Eat a hydrating snack
- Do a cross-lateral movement

Five-Minute Recovery Ideas:

- Take a short walk outside or around the office
- Do a quick body scan to notice and release tension
- Listen to a favorite calming song
- Balanced Brain Breathing
- Brain dump of your thoughts

Fifteen-Minute Recovery Ideas:

- Do a short fascial maneuvers routine
- Watch entertaining videos
- Read a few pages of a book you enjoy
- Step outside for some fresh air and sunlight
- Journal your thoughts or reflect on your day

Creating Your Personal Recovery Menu

Create your own recovery menu by writing down three recovery breaks for each time frame: one minute, five minutes, and fifteen minutes. As we've mentioned repeatedly these should be simple and realistic actions you can commit to doing regularly. Think about how you can remind yourself to take these breaks throughout the day. You might set reminders on your phone or computer, team up with a recovery buddy, use an app, or keep your recovery menu somewhere visible at your desk.

Using your recovery menu with options for one minute, five minute, and fifteen minute breaks means you have a clear plan for how and when to bring recovery into your day. Taking an active approach means planning ahead so that when unexpected moments arise, you can use them to reset immediately without wasting time deciding what to do.

Take a few moments to reflect on the following questions:

Reflection Questions

Which micro-recovery strategies seem most realistic and enjoyable for you?

____

____

How will you remind yourself to take recovery breaks consistently?

____

____

What are the reasons (i.e., excuses) you may choose to justify not taking intentional recovery breaks?

____

____

How will your energy and focus improve when you consistently use your recovery menu?

____

____

Your Recovery Menu is now complete—a living, flexible toolkit of micro-moments that will keep your energy battery topped up even on the most demanding days. These small, repeatable pauses are the foundation of sustainable performance. Yet knowing what to do is only half the equation; the real power comes from choosing one meaningful area to focus on and committing to it consistently. That is exactly what your Micro Mission will give you: a clear, 30-day target that turns insight into habit and habit into identity. With your recovery practices already in place to support you, you are perfectly positioned to take this next focused step. Let's design your Micro Mission now—the single commitment that will move you measurably closer to your Best Self.

17

Clarifying Your Micro Mission

Think of your Micro Mission as your next right step: a focused, intentional goal that you will commit to for the next 30 days.[1,2] Choose just one area we've explored throughout this book. Maybe it's rewriting a limiting story, moving your body more intentionally, allowing yourself deeper rest, or consciously responding to stress in a new way. Once you've chosen your area of focus, connect it to your why. Why does this matter to you now? Who in your life will benefit when you follow through? What part of you is ready to expand? When you tie your mission to a meaningful reason, you're much more likely to stay with it, especially on the harder days.

Today's Date: ________________

The Date 30 Days from Today: ________________

My Area of Focus (WHAT) is. . .

____

____

____

This is Important to me Because (WHY). . .[3,4]

[Who in your life is going to benefit from you focusing on your Micro Mission]

____

____

____

Micro Mission Examples

My area of focus is incorporating more recovery breaks throughout my workday. This is important to me because my spouse and children will benefit the most as I will be more engaging, present, and fun to be around, which will strengthen my relationships with them.

—Jessie

My area of focus is paying closer attention to my emotions throughout the day and when I notice I am in the Stress Response. This is important to me because this will benefit my coworkers so that we can build trusted relationships and I am showing up more consistently as a team member.

—Chris

My area of focus is moving more consistently throughout my workday. This is important to me because this will benefit my community as I will be able to show up more energized to our weekly activities and have a greater impact.

—Blake

18

Impactful Growth Plan

You now have the "what" you want to focus on for the next 30 days and the "why" you want to focus on it. Now you need the "how."

At this point in many personal development books and/or training programs, the "how" is completed with what we refer to as the "Best Case" day in mind. This is a day when everything goes pretty much as you would like. Here is what will likely happen if you only plan for the "Best Case" day. Tomorrow will come and you will have the intention to implement your Micro Mission goal. Then something unexpected happens during the day and, as a result you do not get to engage in your Micro Mission. Then the next day comes and the same type of scenario occurs, and you do not engage in your Micro Mission. By the third day, you start telling yourself, "that stuff in the book doesn't work."

So what is the solution to significantly increase the likelihood of you engaging in your Micro Mission every day?

You need to plan for each type of day you encounter.[1]

We all know that it is relatively easy to take action on your goals when everything is going smoothly (i.e., Best Case day). But growth truly happens in how you show up on the messy days. That's why you need a plan for every kind of day, not just the Best Case days.[2] You need to plan for three types of days[3]:

Take your Micro Mission and ask yourself:

- What will I do when I have a "Best Case" day? (everything goes as planned)
- What is possible on a "Normal" day? (some goes as planned, some goes sideways)
- What is the bare minimum I can do on a "Worst Case" day? (the day wins the moment you wake up)

Planning this way is about developing and maintaining consistency and breaking free from the all-or-nothing mentality. In "pop" psychology, dopamine is often described as the "achievement neurotransmitter," meaning that you work, grind, and push toward some goal and then once you achieve it, you get a flood of dopamine. What's really happening is that by choosing to engage in consistent, intentional action toward your goal, your body releases a bit of dopamine each time, no matter how small that goal-oriented action is. Your brain likes this, and so does your body.[4]

The more consistently you consciously engage in behaviors that align with your Micro Mission (i.e., your rituals), even on the worst-case days, the more you are training your body to release some level of dopamine related to your goal.[5] Your body naturally wants to feel good, so the more frequently you choose to engage in goal-directed actions (your rituals), the easier it becomes to convert those rituals into habits.

Now choose one or two small rituals that support your Micro Mission. Break them down into best, normal, and worst case scenarios (Figure 18.1).

Be specific. The more detailed you are, the less decision-making your future self has to do. Is this ritual specific enough? Is it actionable? Do you feel confident with your rituals? Remember, consistency is the most important element. Doing something, no matter how small, is better than doing nothing. This is how you effectively train a new habit that benefits your quality of life. We have provided some examples in Figure 18.2.

IMPACTFUL GROWTH PLAN

(How will you implement your micro mission?)

	1.	2.
RITUAL		
BEST CASE		
NORMAL		
WORST CASE		

Figure 18.1 Impactful growth plan template.

IMPACTFUL GROWTH PLAN

RITUAL	I will choose to intentionally recover more frequently throughout my day.	I will be more present with my family when I am home.
BEST CASE	I will walk outside around the building for 5 minutes every hour, and I will do Balanced Brain Breathing for at least 2 minutes right before I eat lunch.	At 7 p.m., I will put my phone on Airplane mode, charge it in the closet (out of sight), and not check it for the remainder of the night.
NORMAL	I will walk up and down the stairs from floors 2–4 for 5 minutes every hour and hydrate (food/liquid) every time I walk.	I put my phone in another room during dinner with my family and will turn my phone off at 9 p.m.
WORST CASE	I will take 10 breaths with a slightly longer exhale (than inhale) when I get in my car before I drive home after work.	I will go to another room to check my phone rather than checking it while I'm with my family.

Figure 18.2 Impactful growth plan examples.

Critical Insight from the Classroom

There's a phrase we often use in sessions that usually gets a few raised eyebrows:

"Aim low."

It's not something high performers hear very often.

In most work environments, especially those filled with A-players, the messaging is the opposite: stretch more, push harder, set ambitious targets, go big. That mindset works well for growth goals and performance metrics.

But when it comes to building rituals—especially around recovery and presence—overreaching can quietly sabotage success.

We see it all the time. Someone leaves a session inspired and declares, "I'm going to meditate 30 minutes every morning, journal every night, hit the gym five days a week and never check my phone after 7 p.m."

It lasts three days.

Then real life intervenes. The goal feels too big. The ritual collapses. And the person concludes, "I just don't have the discipline."

That's why we say: aim low.

Small enough that you can't talk yourself out of it.

We worked with one participant whose focus was being more present with her family. She recognized something important: being physically home was not the same as being intentionally engaged. Her body crossed the threshold each evening—but her attention often stayed at work.

Her ritual?

"I'm going to switch my phone all the way off before walking into the house."

Not silent. Not face down. Off.

So simple. So powerful.

That small act removed the temptation to check one more email, finish one more text, glance at one more notification while stepping through the door. It created a clean transition between roles.

Why does this matter so much?

Because how you enter a room communicates everything.

If you walk into your home—or any room—with your phone up and your head down, the message is unmistakable: whatever is on this screen is more important than the people in front of me.

Even if that's not your intention, it's the signal you send.

When you walk in with no phone in hand, eyes up, attention available, the message flips: you have my full presence.

That's not just symbolic. It's relational.

Attention is one of the most powerful currencies in human connection. And presence doesn't require a grand gesture. It requires removing friction.

Her ritual didn't demand more time. It didn't require extra effort. It simply eliminated distraction at a critical transition point.

That's what "aim low" really means.

Choose a behavior so small, so clear, and so doable that it becomes automatic. Success builds momentum. Momentum builds identity. Identity sustains change.

In high-performance cultures, we're trained to think bigger is better.

But when it comes to rituals that protect your Best Self, small and consistent beats ambitious and abandoned every time.

19

Your Environment

Your Micro Mission becomes part of who you are through repetition, not pressure. It's not about being extraordinary every day. It's about doing something even when you don't feel like it.

And that's where your environment comes in.

Your environment plays a powerful role in discovering and staying in your Best Self. This isn't just about the physical spaces around you like your home, office, or neighborhood, but also the people you spend time with, the routines you follow and even the sounds and smells that surround you. These factors act as constant cues to your brain, influencing your thoughts, emotions, and behaviors, often without you realizing it through a process called classical conditioning.

Pavlovian conditioning, or classical conditioning, is when a neutral stimulus becomes associated with a response through repeated pairing.[1] For example, if you always hear a certain song while working out, that song eventually triggers your brain to prepare for exercise, boosting your brain to release energy chemicals into your body even if you are simply sitting on your couch at the time. Similarly, by intentionally designing your environment with positive cues, you can train your brain to respond with focus, calm or energy, helping you stay consistent and grow.[2]

Imagine you want to develop a daily meditation habit to manage stress. If your environment is cluttered or noisy, it can be harder to relax. But if you create a dedicated space with a cushion, soft lighting, and calming scents, through consistent repetition these sensory cues become associated with calm and mindfulness.[3] Over time, just entering that space signals your nervous system to shift into a more relaxed state automatically, making meditation easier and more inviting even on challenging days.

The people around you also serve as powerful environmental cues. Spending time with supportive friends or colleagues who value growth can reinforce your own motivation and commitment.[4] Their attitudes and behaviors act as social signals that condition you to adopt similar mindsets and habits. Conversely, negative influences can condition doubt or lethargy, making it harder to stay on track.

Reflection Questions

What environmental cues at home and at work currently signal your Best Self to show up? What specific sights, sounds, or people consistently put you in a more open, growth-oriented state?

____

____

____

How will you intentionally add new cues to your environment that signal growth, focus, or calm? What small changes will you make to support your habits?

____

____

____

Remember a time when a certain place or routine automatically helped you feel motivated or peaceful. How will you recreate or expand on those conditions today?

____

____

____

Creating Your Best Self Environment

Take 10 minutes to walk through your daily spaces, your home, workspace, or wherever you spend a lot of time. Notice the things that support your focus, calm, or energy, as well as the things that distract or drain you. Ask yourself:

What will I remove or reduce that doesn't serve my growth?

What small additions (a plant, a reminder note, a diffuser, or a photo) will function as positive cues for my goals?

Who around me supports the person I am going to become? How will I spend more quality time with those people or involve them in my growth?

Write down 2–3 concrete changes you can make this week to better align your environment with your Best Self. Then commit to observing over the next few days how these changes impact your mood, motivation, and habits.

By shaping your environment intentionally, you are setting the stage for lasting growth and making it easier for your brain and body to show up as your Best Self every day. By understanding and harnessing the impact of environmental cues, you can design your surroundings to support impactful growth naturally and effortlessly. This is about working with your brain's wiring, not against it, so growth becomes a smooth, integrated part of your daily life.

Real, lasting change rarely happens in isolation. Growth is most sustainable when it's supported by both inner clarity and the environment around you. That includes the people you surround yourself with, the systems you create, and the spaces you move through each day.

To move forward with intention, you don't need to overhaul your entire life at once. You just need to begin and keep going.

Rewiring Through Repetition

If you want to become someone who follows through on your growth, place yourself around people who already embody that. Observe them. Learn from them. Let their behavior become a mirror and a model. As the saying goes: If you want to build habits that last, join a group where your desired behavior is the norm.

Think about this:

What are the signs that you're growing?

____

____

____

Who in your life is already living the way you want to live?

____

____

____

How can you learn from them, model them or even simply spend more time in their presence?

____

____

____

Write it down. Say it out loud. Bring it to life.

Conclusion: Live It Forward

THE FACT THAT you've made it this far means you've done more than just read a book! You've started to open up to a new way of living and leading. You've met the two versions of yourself: the Stressed Self that often runs the show unnoticed, and the Best Self that is wise, calm, capable, and deeply alive. You've explored how stress affects your biology, mindset, behaviors, and relationships and, more importantly, how it can be transformed, not avoided or suppressed, but worked with in ways that restore energy, deepen purpose, and elevate performance.

This book was never about achieving perfection or eliminating all stress. That's not realistic, and it's not the goal. Instead, it's about building awareness, creating margin, and learning to shift from reactive to responsive. It's about reclaiming your ability to choose, how you breathe, move, think, speak, rest, connect, and lead.

We've given you science-backed tools and real-life strategies to rewire how you respond to pressure, how you care for yourself, and how you show up in the world. But tools are only as powerful as your willingness to use them. Awareness is powerful. Action is transformative. And repetition, small, consistent shifts, is what rewires your nervous system and rewrites your story.

So, where do you go from here?

You start again. Each day, each moment, is an opportunity to return to your Best Self, even if you've strayed for hours or weeks. Your Stressed Self will still show up, and that's okay. Now you recognize it. Now you have the tools. Now you have the choice.

Whether you are leading a team, raising a family, building a business, or simply trying to stay grounded in an increasingly fast-paced world, the invitation is the same: Don't just survive. Choose to flourish.

You are capable of more ease, more clarity, more connection, and more impact, not by doing more, but by aligning more. Aligning with your values, your energy, your purpose, and the version of you that already knows how to lead from a grounded, empowered place.

This is just the beginning. Your life doesn't have to feel like a fight against time, stress, or exhaustion. There is a better way, and you've just unlocked it.

Now take what you've learned, choose to train it every day, and live it forward.

And remember to always. . .pause and think before you react.

—Kevin & Nick

Impact Human Performance

References

Introduction: The Two Versions of You

1. American Psychological Association. (2018, November 1; last reviewed October 21, 2024). Stress effects on the body. https://www.apa.org/topics/stress/body (developed with contributions from William Shaw, PhD; Susan Labott-Smith, PhD, ABPP; Matthew M. Burg, PhD; Camelia Hostinar, PhD).
2. Mayo Clinic. (2023, August 10). Stress symptoms: Effects on your body and behavior. https://www.mayoclinic.org/healthy-lifestyle/stress-management/in-depth/stress-symptoms/art-20050987
3. World Health Organization. (2019, May 28). "Burn-out an occupational phenomenon": International Classification of Diseases. https://www.who.int/news/item/28-05-2019-burn-out-an-occupational-phenomenon-international-classification-of-diseases
4. Van Dam, A., et al. (2025). Chronic stress in relation to clinical burnout: An integrative scoping review of definitions and measurement approaches. *Frontiers in Psychology*. https://www.frontiersin.org/journals/psychology/articles/10.3389/fpsyg.2025.1712340/full
5. American Psychological Association. (2017). Stress in America™: The state of our nation. https://www.apa.org/news/press/releases/stress/2017/state-nation.pdf

6. Gallup. (2025). *State of the Global Workplace: 2025 Report.* https://www.gallup.com/workplace/349484/state-of-the-global-workplace.aspx
7. TherapyRoute. (2025). *Workplace stress and burnout: 2025 statistics.*
8. Al-Mansour, M. A., et al. (2025). Write to heal: The impact of an expressive writing intervention on stress in first-year nursing students. *BMC Nursing* (PMC). https://pmc.ncbi.nlm.nih.gov/articles/PMC12866060/

Chapter 2: What Happens When You're Stressed?

1. Yaribeygi, H., Panahi, Y., Sahraei, H., Johnston, T. P., & Sahebkar, A. (2017). The impact of stress on body function: A review. *EXCLI Journal, 16*, 1057–1072. https://doi.org/10.17179/excli2017-480
2. Dhabhar, F. S. (2018). The short-term stress response – Mother Nature's mechanism for enhancing protection and performance under conditions of threat, challenge, and opportunity. *Frontiers in Neuroendocrinology*, *49*, 175–192. https://doi.org/10.1016/j.yfrne.2018.03.001
3. Valencia-Florez, K. B., Sánchez-Castillo, H., Vázquez, P., Zarate, P., & Paz, D. B. (2023). Stress, a brief update. *International Journal of Psychological Research, 16(2)*, 105–121. https://doi.org/10.21500/20112084.5815
4. Girotti, M., Bulin, S. E., & Carreno, F. R. (2024). Effects of chronic stress on cognitive function – From neurobiology to intervention. *Neurobiology of Stress*, *33*, Article 100670. https://doi.org/10.1016/j.ynstr.2024.100670
5. LeWine, H. E. (2024, April 3). Understanding the stress response. *Harvard Health Publishing.* https://www.health.harvard.edu/staying-healthy/understanding-the-stress-response

Chapter 3: Recognizing Your Stressed Self in Action

1. Price, C. J., & Hooven, C. (2018). Interoceptive awareness skills for emotion regulation: Theory and approach of mindful awareness in body-oriented therapy (MABT). *Frontiers in Psychology*, 9, Article 798. https://doi.org/10.3389/fpsyg.2018.00798
2. Coates, D., Lewis, S., & Burge-Ferrow, G. (2025). The relationship between interoception and experiences of stress, trauma, and mental illness: A scoping review. *Psychotherapy and Counselling Journal of Australia, 13(2)*. https://doi.org/10.59158/001c.146359

3. Garfinkel, S. N., & Eccleston, C. (2025). Interoception and pain: Body–mind integration, rupture, and repair. *PAIN*, *166(7)*, 1470–1474. https://doi.org/10.1097/j.pain.0000000000003515
4. Attia, M., Ibrahim, F. A., Elsady, M. A.-E., Khorkhash, M. K., Rizk, M. A., Shah, J., & Amer, S. A. (2022). Cognitive, emotional, physical, and behavioral stress-related symptoms and coping strategies among university students during the third wave of COVID-19 pandemic. *Frontiers in Psychiatry*, *13*, Article 933981. https://doi.org/10.3389/fpsyt.2022.933981
5. Jenkins, K., Buchan, J., Rhodes, R. E., & Hamilton, K. (2024). Exploring environmental cues to instigate physical movement in the workplace. *Health Psychology and Behavioral Medicine*, *12(1)*, Article 2323433. https://doi.org/10.1080/21642850.2024.2323433
6. Montoya, R. M., Horton, R. S., Vevea, J. L., Citkowicz, M., & Lauber, E. A. (2017). A re-examination of the mere exposure effect: The influence of repeated exposure on recognition, familiarity, and liking. *Psychological Bulletin*, *143(5)*, 459–498. https://doi.org/10.1037/bul0000085

Chapter 4: Your Gateway to Change

1. Ferrari, M., Hunt, C., Harrysunker, A., Abbott, M. J., Beath, A. P., & Einstein, D. A. (2019). Self-compassion interventions and psychosocial outcomes: A meta-analysis of RCTs. *Mindfulness*, *10(8)*, 1455–1473. https://doi.org/10.1007/s12671-019-01134-6
2. Eriksson, T., Germundsjö, L., Åström, E., & Rönnlund, M. (2018). Mindful self-compassion training reduces stress and burnout symptoms among practicing psychologists: A randomized controlled trial of a brief web-based intervention. *Frontiers in Psychology*, *9*, Article 2340. https://doi.org/10.3389/fpsyg.2018.02340
3. Andrade, H. L., & Brookhart, S. M. (2021). Classroom assessment as co-regulated learning: A systematic review. *Frontiers in Education*, *6*, Article 751168. https://doi.org/10.3389/feduc.2021.751168
4. Falon, S. L., Kangas, M., & Crane, M. F. (2021). The coping insights involved in strengthening resilience: The self-reflection and coping insight framework. *Anxiety, Stress & Coping*, *34(6)*, 734–750. https://doi.org/10.1080/10.15806.2021.1910676
5. Falon, S. L., Hoare, S., Kangas, M., & Crane, M. F. (2022). The coping insights evident through self-reflection on stressful military training

events: Qualitative evidence from self-reflection journals. *Stress and Health*, *38*(5), 902–918. https://doi.org/10.1002/smi.3141
6. Zangri, R. M., Andreu, C. I., Nieto, I., González-Garzón, A. M., & Vázquez, C. (2022). Efficacy of mindfulness to regulate induced emotions in the laboratory: A systematic review and meta-analysis of self-report and biobehavioral measures. *Neuroscience & Biobehavioral Reviews*, *143*, Article 104957. https://doi.org/10.1016/j.neubiorev.2022.104957

Chapter 5: Meeting and Unlocking Your Best Self

1. Carrillo, A., Rubio-Aparicio, M., Molinari, G., Enrique, Á., Sánchez-Meca, J., & Baños, R. M. (2019). Effects of the Best Possible Self intervention: A systematic review and meta-analysis. *PLOS ONE*, *14*(9), Article e0222386. https://doi.org/10.1371/journal.pone.0222386
2. Stackpole, A. R., Crane, M. F., Riddell, H., & [co-authors]. (2026). Event-informed systematic self-reflections and stress reactivity among emerging adults: Insights from an ecological momentary assessment experiment. *Stress and Health*, *42*(1), Article e70150. https://doi.org/10.1002/smi.70150
3. Holt-Lunstad, J. (2022). Social connection as a public health issue: The evidence and a systemic framework for prioritizing the "social" in social determinants of health. *Annual Review of Public Health*, *43*, 193–213. https://doi.org/10.1146/annurev-publhealth-052020-110732
4. Holt-Lunstad, J. (2024). Social connection as a critical factor for mental and physical health: Evidence, trends, challenges, and future implications. *World Psychiatry*, *23*(3), 312–332. https://doi.org/10.1002/wps.21224
5. Verplanken, B., Roy, D., & Whitmarsh, L. (2020). What influences the selection of contextual cues when starting a new routine behaviour? An exploratory study. *Psychology & Health*. Advance online publication. https://doi.org/10.1080/08870446.2020.1724339
6. van Vianen, A. E. M. (2018). Person–environment fit: A review of its basic tenets. *Annual Review of Organizational Psychology and Organizational Behavior*, *5*, 75–101. https://doi.org/10.1146/annurev-orgpsych-032117-104702
7. Curran, T., & Hill, A. P. (2019). Perfectionism is increasing over time: A meta-analysis of birth cohort differences from 1989 to 2016. *Psychological Bulletin*, *145*(4), 410–429. https://doi.org/10.1037/bul0000138
8. Flett, G. L., & Hewitt, P. L. (2022). The destructiveness and public health significance of socially prescribed perfectionism: A review,

analysis, and conceptual extension. *Clinical Psychology Review*, *93*, Article 102130. https://doi.org/10.1016/j.cpr.2022.10.130

9. Tanovic, E., Gee, D. G., & Joormann, J. (2018). Intolerance of uncertainty: Neural and psychophysiological correlates of the perception of uncertainty as threatening. *Clinical Psychology Review*, *60*, 87–99. https://doi.org/10.1016/j.cpr.2018.01.001

Chapter 6: Barriers to Being Your Best Self

1. Jacoby, R., Greenfeld Barsky, K., Porat, T., Harel, S., Hanalis Miller, T., & Goldzweig, G. (2021). Individual stress response patterns: Preliminary findings and possible implications. *PLoS ONE*, *16*(8), Article e0255889. https://doi.org/10.1371/journal.pone.0255889
2. Polsky, L. R., Rentscher, K. E., & Carroll, J. E. (2022). Stress-induced biological aging: A review and guide for research priorities. *Brain, Behavior, and Immunity*, *104*, 97–109. https://doi.org/10.1016/j.bbi.2022.05.016
3. Levit-Binnun, N., Arbel, K., & Dorjee, D. (2021). The Mindfulness Map: A practical classification framework of mindfulness practices, associated intentions, and experiential understandings. *Frontiers in Psychology*, *12*, Article 727857. https://doi.org/10.3389/fpsyg.2021.727857
4. Curtiss, J. E., Levine, D. S., Ander, I., & Baker, A. W. (2021). Cognitive-behavioral treatments for anxiety and stress-related disorders. *Focus*, *19*(2), 184–189. https://doi.org/10.1176/appi.focus.20200045
5. Berkman, E. T. (2018). The neuroscience of goals and behavior change. *Consulting Psychology Journal: Practice and Research*, *70*(1), 28–44. https://doi.org/10.1037/cpb0000094
6. da Silva, L. A., et al. (2022). The impact of a brief mindfulness training on interoception: A randomized controlled trial. *PLoS ONE*, *17*(9), Article e0273864

Chapter 7: Regulating Your Emotions

1. Kraiss, J. T., ten Klooster, P. M., Moskowitz, J. T., & Bohlmeijer, E. T. (2020). The relationship between emotion regulation and well-being in patients with mental disorders: A meta-analysis. *Comprehensive Psychiatry*, *102*, Article 152189. https://doi.org/10.1016/j.comppsych.2020.152189

2. Porges, S. W. (2022). Polyvagal theory: A science of safety. *Frontiers in Integrative Neuroscience*, *16*, Article 871227. https://doi.org/10.3389/fnint.2022.871227
3. Harris, D. J., Allen, K. L., Vine, S. J., & Wilson, M. R. (2021). A systematic review and meta-analysis of the relationship between flow states and performance. *International Review of Sport and Exercise Psychology*, *16*(1), 693–721.
4. Vandenabeele, R., Joosen, M. C. W., & van Dam, A. (2025). Chronic stress in relation to clinical burnout: An integrative scoping review of definitions and measurement approaches. *Frontiers in Psychology*, *16*, Article 1712340. https://doi.org/10.3389/fpsyg.2025.1712340
5. Albulescu, P., Macsinga, I., Rusu, A., Sulea, C., Bodnaru, A., & Tulbure, B. T. (2022). "Give me a break!" A systematic review and meta-analysis on the efficacy of micro-breaks for increasing well-being and performance. *PLoS ONE*, *17*(8), Article e0272460. https://doi.org/10.1371/journal.pone.0272460
6. Bennett, A. A., Bakker, A. B., & Field, J. G. (2018). Recovery from work-related effort: A meta-analysis. *Journal of Organizational Behavior*, *39*(3), 262–275. https://doi.org/10.1002/job.2217

Chapter 8: Defining Intentional Recovery

1. Albulescu, P., Macsinga, I., Sulea, C., Pap, Z., Tulbure, B. T., & Rusu, A. (2025). Short breaks during the workday and employee-related outcomes: A diary study. *Psychological Reports*. https://doi.org/10.1177/00332941251317632
2. Sonnentag, S., Cheng, B. H., & Parker, S. L. (2022). Recovery from work: Advancing the field toward the future. *Annual Review of Organizational Psychology and Organizational Behavior*, 9, 33–60. https://doi.org/10.1146/annurev-orgpsych-012420-091355
3. Albulescu, P., Macsinga, I., Rusu, A., Sulea, C., Bodnaru, A., & Tulbure, B. T. (2022). "Give me a break!" A systematic review and meta-analysis on the efficacy of micro-breaks for increasing well-being and performance. *PLoS ONE*, *17*(8), Article e0272460. https://doi.org/10.1371/journal.pone.0272460
4. Phan, V., & Beck, J. W. (2023). Why do people (not) take breaks? An investigation of individuals' reasons for taking and for not taking breaks at work. *Journal of Business and Psychology*, *38*(2), 259–282. https://doi.org/10.1007/s10869-022-09866-4

5. Sianoja, M., Syrek, C. J., de Bloom, J., Korpela, K., & Kinnunen, U. (2018). Enhancing daily well-being at work through lunchtime park walks and relaxation exercises: Recovery experiences as mediators. *Journal of Occupational Health Psychology*, *23*(3), 428–442. https://doi.org/10.1037/ocp0000083

Chapter 9: A New Way Forward

1. Parker, S. L., Zacher, H., de Bloom, J., & Verton, T. M. (2017). Daily use of energy management strategies and occupational well-being: The moderating role of job demands. *Frontiers in Psychology*, 8, Article 1477. https://doi.org/10.3389/fpsyg.2017.01477
2. Pladdys, J. (2024). Mitigating workplace burnout through transformational leadership and employee participation in recovery experiences. *HCA Healthcare Journal of Medicine*, *5*(3), 215–223. https://doi.org/10.36518/2689-0216.1783
3. Albulescu, P., Macsinga, I., Rusu, A., Sulea, C., Bodnaru, A., & Tulbure, B. T. (2022). "Give me a break!" A systematic review and meta-analysis on the efficacy of micro-breaks for increasing well-being and performance. *PLoS ONE*, *17*(8), Article e0272460. https://doi.org/10.1371/journal.pone.0272460
4. Sonnentag, S., Cheng, B. H., & Parker, S. L. (2022). Recovery from work: Advancing the field toward the future. *Annual Review of Organizational Psychology and Organizational Behavior*, 9, 33–60. https://doi.org/10.1146/annurev-orgpsych-012420-091355
5. Porges, S. W. (2022). Polyvagal theory: A science of safety. *Frontiers in Integrative Neuroscience*, *16*, Article 871227. https://doi.org/10.3389/fnint.2022.871227
6. Curtiss, J. E., Levine, D. S., Ander, I., & Baker, A. W. (2021). Cognitive-behavioral treatments for anxiety and stress-related disorders. *Focus*, *19*(2), 184–189. https://doi.org/10.1176/appi.focus.20200045
7. Weyland, S., Fritsch, J., Feil, K., & Jekauc, D. (2022). Investigating the relation between positive affective responses and exercise instigation habits in an affect-based intervention for exercise trainers: A longitudinal field study. *Frontiers in Psychology*, *13*, Article 994177. https://doi.org/10.3389/fpsyg.2022.994177
8. Naczenski, L. M., de Vries, J. D., van Hooff, M. L. M., & Kompier, M. A. J. (2017). Systematic review of the association between physical activity and burnout. *Journal of Occupational Health*, 59(6), 477–494. https://doi.org/10.1539/joh.17-0050-RA

9. Fincham, G. W., Strauss, C., Montero-Marin, J., & Cavanagh, K. (2023). Effect of breathwork on stress and mental health: A meta-analysis of randomised-controlled trials. *Scientific Reports, 13*(1), Article 432. https://doi.org/10.1038/s41598-022-27247-y
10. Zhang, N., Du, S. M., Zhang, J. F., & Ma, G. S. (2019). Effects of dehydration and rehydration on cognitive performance and mood among male college students in Cangzhou, China: A self-controlled trial. *International Journal of Environmental Research and Public Health, 16*(11), Article 1891. https://doi.org/10.3390/ijerph16111891
11. Chu, B., Marwaha, K., Sanvictores, T., Awosika, A., & Ayers, D. (2025/updated 2024). Physiology, stress reaction. In *StatPearls*. National Library of Medicine.
12. Wang, Y., Vlemincx, E., Vantieghem, I., Dhar, M., Dong, D., & Vandekerckhove, M. (2022). Bottom-up and cognitive top-down emotion regulation: Experiential emotion regulation and cognitive reappraisal on stress relief and follow-up sleep physiology. *International Journal of Environmental Research and Public Health, 19*(13), Article 7621. https://doi.org/10.3390/ijerph19137621

Chapter 10: Moving to Thrive

1. Gao, W., Sanna, M., Chen, Y., Tsai, M., & Wen, C. (2024). Occupational sitting time, leisure physical activity, and all-cause and cardiovascular disease mortality. *JAMA Network Open, 7*(1), Article e2350680. https://doi.org/10.1001/jamanetworkopen.2023.50680
2. Li, K., Zhao, Y., Mo, H., & Li, Y. (2024). Association between long-term sedentary behavior and depressive symptoms in U.S. adults. *Scientific Reports, 14*, Article 5247. https://doi.org/10.1038/s41598-024-55898-6
3. Park, J. H., Moon, J. H., Kim, H. J., Kong, M. H., & Oh, Y. H. (2020). Sedentary lifestyle: Overview of updated evidence of potential health risks. *Korean Journal of Family Medicine, 41*(6), 365–373. https://doi.org/10.4082/kjfm.20.0165 (PMC7700832)
4. Owen, N., Sugiyama, T., Eakin, E. E., Gardiner, P. A., Tremblay, M. S., & Sallis, J. F. (2011). Adults' sedentary behavior determinants and interventions. *American Journal of Preventive Medicine, 41*(2), 189–196. https://doi.org/10.1016/j.amepre.2011.04.013
5. Barr-Anderson, D. J., AuYoung, M., Whitt-Glover, M. C., Glenn, B. A., & Yancey, A. K. (2011). Integration of short bouts of physical activity into organizational routine: A systematic review of the literature.

American Journal of Preventive Medicine, 40(1), 76–93. https://doi.org/10.1016/j.amepre.2010.09.033

6. Almendras, M., & Peper, E. (2021). Reactivate your second heart. *Biofeedback*, 49(4), 99–102.
7. McBane, R. D., et al. (2024). Calf rEF: Impact of calf muscle pump dysfunction with reduced ejection fraction on all-cause mortality. *Mayo Clinic Proceedings*, 99(6), 902–912.
8. Hamilton, M. T., Hamilton, D. G., & Zderic, T. W. (2022). Soleus push-up: A potent exercise for improving metabolic health. *iScience*, 25(10), 105087.
9. Orr, L., Klement, K. A., McCrossin, L., O'Sullivan Drombolis, D., Houghton, P. E., Spaulding, S., & Burke, S. (2017). A systematic review and meta-analysis of exercise intervention for the treatment of calf muscle pump impairment in individuals with chronic venous insufficiency. *Ostomy Wound Management*, 63(8), 30–43.
10. Tömörkènyi, M. *Human Mechanics: Unleashing the Potential of a Highly Advanced Species*. DBC A/S, 2022.
11. Ocklenburg, S., Packheiser, J., & Schmitz, J. (2024). Cross-hemispheric communication: Insights on lateralized brain functions. *Neuron*, 112(7), 1036–1053. https://doi.org/10.1016/j.neuron.2024.02.010
12. Dreisoerner, A., Junker, N. M., Schlotz, W., Heimrich, J., Bloemeke, S., Ditzen, B., & van Dick, R. (2021). Self-soothing touch and being hugged reduce cortisol responses to stress: A randomized controlled trial on stress, physical touch, and social identity. *Comprehensive Psychoneuroendocrinology*, 8, Article 100091. https://doi.org/10.1016/j.cpnec.2021.100091
13. von Au, S., Marsh, N., Jeske, V., Hurlemann, R., & Lausberg, H. (2025). Effects of self-touch and social-touch on peripheral oxytocin concentrations: A study conducted during the COVID-19 pandemic. *Physiology & Behavior*, 115061. https://doi.org/10.1016/j.physbeh.2025.115061
14. Susanti, Y., Candra, E. L., & Anggraeni, R. (2025). The effect of self-healing butterfly hug on anxiety levels. *Journal of Nursing Practice*, 8(2), 407–418. https://doi.org/10.30994/jnp.v8i2.668
15. Dunville, L. M., Sood, G., & Kramer, J. Oculocardiac Reflex. In: *StatPearls*. Treasure Island (FL): StatPearls Publishing; 2024 May 7 (updated)
16. Wu, B.-Q., Kuo, H.-T., Hsu, A. Y., Lin, C.-J., Lai, C.-T., & Tsai, Y.-Y. (2024). The clinical efficacy of different relaxation exercises on

intraocular pressure: A systematic review and meta-analysis. *Journal of Clinical Medicine, 13(9)*, 2591. https://doi.org/10.3390/jcm13092591

17. Papalia, G. F. et al. (2020). The effects of physical exercise on balance and prevention of falls in older people: A systematic review and meta-analysis. *International Journal of Environmental Research and Public Health, 17(16)*, 6003. https://doi.org/10.3390/ijerph17166003

Chapter 11: Hydrating Your Way to Increased Energy

1. Kavouras, S. A., & Murad, H. (2021). *Hydration Science and Strategies.* Human Kinetics.
2. Kavouras, S. A. (2019). Hydration, dehydration, underhydration, optimal hydration: Are we barking up the wrong tree? *European Journal of Nutrition, 58(2)*, 471–473.
3. Dmitrieva, N. I., Boehm, M., Yancey, P. H., & Enhörning, S. (2024). Long-term health outcomes associated with hydration status. *Nature Reviews Nephrology, 20(5)*, 275–294.
4. Kavouras, S. A., et al. (2018). Dehydration impairs performance, regardless of thirst. *Medicine & Science in Sports & Exercise, 50(8)*, 1697–1703.
5. Slater, A. M., Barclay, S. J., Granfar, R. M. S., & Pratt, R. L. (2024). Fascia as a regulatory system in health and disease. *Frontiers in Neurology, 15*, 1458385. https://doi.org/10.3389/fneur.2024.1458385
6. Zhang, N., Du, S. M., Zhang, J. F., & Ma, G. S. (2019). Effects of dehydration and rehydration on cognitive performance and mood among male college students in Cangzhou, China: A self-controlled trial. *International Journal of Environmental Research and Public Health, 16(11)*, 1891. https://doi.org/10.3390/ijerph16111891
7. Trangmar, S. J., & González-Alonso, J. (2019). Heat, hydration and the human brain, heart and skeletal muscles. *Sports Medicine*, 49(Suppl 1), 69–85. https://doi.org/10.1007/s40279-018-1033-y
8. Shrimanker, I., et al. (2023). Electrolytes. In StatPearls. NCBI Bookshelf.
9. Kavouras, S. A., & Murad, H. (2021). *Hydration Science and Strategies.* Human Kinetics.
10. Matek Sarić, M., et al. (2025). Magnesium: Health effects, deficiency burden, and future public health directions. *Nutrients, 17(22)*, 3626. https://doi.org/10.3390/nu17223626
11. Pirahanchi, Y., et al. (2023). Physiology, Sodium Potassium Pump. In *StatPearls*. Treasure Island (FL): StatPearls Publishing.

12. Touyz, R. M., et al. (2024). Magnesium Disorders. In Endotext [Internet]. South Dartmouth (MA): MDText.com, Inc.
13. Bhardwaj, R. L., et al. (2024). An alarming decline in the nutritional quality of foods: The biggest challenge for future generations' health. *Cureus, 16(3)*, e56789.
14. Périard, J. D., et al. (2021). Exercise under heat stress: Thermoregulation, hydration, performance implications, and mitigation strategies. *Physiological Reviews, 101(4)*, 1907–1989. https://doi.org/10.1152/physrev.00038.2020
15. Armstrong, L. E. (2021). Rehydration during endurance exercise: Challenges, research, options, methods. *Nutrients, 13(3)*, 1002. https://doi.org/10.3390/nu13031002
16. Pollack, G. H. (2013). *The Fourth Phase of Water: Beyond Solid, Liquid, and Vapor*. Ebner & Sons Publishers. ISBN 978-0962689543
17. Elton, D. C., Spencer, P. D., Riches, J. D., & Williams, E. D. (2020). Exclusion zone phenomena in water—A critical review of experimental findings and theories. *International Journal of Molecular Sciences, 21(14)*, 5041. https://doi.org/10.3390/ijms21145041
18. Slater, A. M., Barclay, S. J., Granfar, R. M. S., & Pratt, R. L. (2024). Fascia as a regulatory system in health and disease. *Frontiers in Neurology, 15*, 1458385.
19. Blottner, D., et al. (2019). The fascia: Continuum linking bone and myofascial bag for global and local body movement control on Earth and in Space. A scoping review. *REACH - Reviews in Human Space Exploration, 14*, 100030. https://doi.org/10.1016/j.reach.2019.100030

Chapter 12: Breathing Your Way to Calm and Focused

1. Laborde, S., Allen, M. S., Borges, U., Dosseville, F., Hosang, T. J., Iskra, M., Javelle, F. (2022). Effects of voluntary slow breathing on heart rate and heart rate variability: A systematic review and a meta-analysis. *Neuroscience & Biobehavioral Reviews, 138*, 104711. https://doi.org/10.1016/j.neubiorev.2022.104711
2. Magnon, V., Dutheil, F., & Vallet, G. T. (2021). Benefits from one session of deep and slow breathing on vagal tone and anxiety in young and older adults. *Scientific Reports, 11*, 19267. https://doi.org/10.1038/s41598-021-98736-9
3. Balban, M. Y., Neri, E., Kogon, M., Weed, L., Tuzel, N., Huberman, A. D., & Spiegel, D. (2023). Brief structured respiration practices enhance

mood and reduce physiological arousal. *Cell Reports Medicine*, 4(1), 100895.
4. Kromenacker, B. W., & Meuret, A. E. (2023). Dysfunctional breathing in chronic fatigue syndrome. *Frontiers in Medicine*, *10*, 1669036.
5. Telles, S., Gupta, R. K., Yadav, A., Pathak, S., & Balkrishna, A. (2017). Hemisphere specific EEG related to alternate nostril yoga breathing. *BMC Research Notes*, *10*, 306. https://doi.org/10.1186/s13104-017-2625-6
6. Sinha, A. N., Deepak, D., & Gusain, V. S. (2013). Assessment of the effects of pranayama/alternate nostril breathing on the parasympathetic nervous system in young adults. *Journal of Clinical and Diagnostic Research*, *7*(12), 2604–2606. https://doi.org/10.7860/JCDR/2013/4750.2948
7. Vanutelli, M. E., Grigis, C., & Lucchiari, C. (2024). Breathing right. . . or left! The effects of unilateral nostril breathing on psychological and cognitive wellbeing: A pilot study. *Brain Sciences*, *14*(4), 302. https://doi.org/10.3390/brainsci14040302
8. Niazi, I. K., et al. (2022). EEG signatures change during unilateral yogi nasal breathing. *Scientific Reports*, *12*(1), 520. https://doi.org/10.1038/s41598-021-04461-8
9. Sinha, M., et al. (2020). Impact of altered breathing patterns on interaction of EEG and heart rate variability. *Indian Journal of Psychological Medicine* (PMC7724429)
10. De Couck, M., et al. (2019). How breathing can help you make better decisions. *International Journal of Psychophysiology*, *139*, 1–9.

Chapter 13: Sleeping Your Way to the Safety Signal

1. Zielinski, M. R., McKenna, J. T., & McCarley, R. W. (2016). Functions and mechanisms of sleep. *AIMS Neuroscience*, *3*(1), 67–104.
2. Louveau, A., Herz, J., Alme, M. N., Salvador, A. F., Dong, M. Q., Viar, K. E., & Kipnis, J. (2017). Understanding the functions and relationships of the glymphatic system and meningeal lymphatics. *Journal of Clinical Investigation*, *127*(9), 3210–3219.
3. Klinzing, J. G., Niethard, N., & Born, J. (2023). Sleep—A brain-state serving systems memory consolidation. *Neuron*, *111*(7), 1050–1075. https://doi.org/10.1016/j.neuron.2023.02.005
4. Ishida, K., et al. (2022). Glymphatic system clears extracellular tau and protects from tau aggregation and neurodegeneration. *Journal of Experimental Medicine*, *219*(3), e20211275.
5. Tempesta, D., Socci, V., De Gennaro, L., & Ferrara, M. (2021). The effect of sleep deprivation and restriction on mood, emotion, and

emotion regulation: Three meta-analyses in one. *Sleep Medicine Reviews*, 59, 101448.

6. Jessen, N. A., Munk, A. S. F., Lundgaard, I., & Nedergaard, M. (2016). The glymphatic system: A beginner's guide. *Neurochemical Research*, 40(12), 2583–2599.
7. Irwin, M. R., & Opp, M. R. (2019). Sleep and immune function. *Pflügers Archiv - European Journal of Physiology*, *471*(11–12), 1411–1423.
8. Besedovsky, L., Lange, T., & Haack, M. (2019). The sleep-immune crosstalk in health and disease. *Physiological Reviews*, 99(3), 1325–1380.
9. Moieni, M., et al. (2019). Exploring the role of gratitude and support-giving on inflammatory outcomes. *Emotion*, *19*(6), 939–949.
10. Kyeong, S., Kim, J., Kim, D. J., Kim, H. E., & Kim, J. J. (2017). Effects of gratitude meditation on neural network functional connectivity and brain-heart coupling. *Scientific Reports*, *7*(1), 5058.
11. Moore, W. E., & Harbaugh, W. T. (2020). The cultivation of pure altruism via gratitude: A functional MRI study of change with gratitude practice. *Frontiers in Human Neuroscience*, *14*, 599164.

Chapter 14: Managing Stressors

1. Ghasemi, F., Beversdorf, D. Q., & Herman, K. C. (2024). Stress and stress responses: A narrative literature review from physiological mechanisms to intervention approaches. *International Journal of School & Educational Psychology*. 10.1177/18344909241289222
2. Vandenabeele, R., Joosen, M. C. W., & van Dam, A. (2025). Chronic stress in relation to clinical burnout: An integrative scoping review of definitions and measurement approaches. *Frontiers in Psychology*, *16*, Article 1712340. https://doi.org/10.3389/fpsyg.2025.1712340
3. Botha, F., & Dahmann, S. C. (2023). Locus of control, self-control, and health outcomes. *SSM – Population Health*, *25*, Article 101566. https://doi.org/10.1016/j.ssmph.2023.101566
4. Stillman, S., et al. (2025). The sensitivity of locus of control to life events and implications for its moderating influence on wellbeing. *Scientific Reports*, *15*, Article 13930. https://doi.org/10.1038/s41598-025-13930-3
5. Meier, J., et al. (2026). Perceived control as a resilience factor: Associations with neural, physiological and affective stress responses and mental health. *Translational Psychiatry*, *16*, Article 39. https://doi.org/10.1038/s41398-025-03786-6
6. Ghasemi, F., Beversdorf, D. Q., & Herman, K. C. (2024). Stress and stress responses: A narrative literature review from physiological mechanisms

to intervention approaches. *Journal of Pacific Rim Psychology, 18*, Article e18344909241289222. https://doi.org/10.1177/18344909241289222
7. Liang, J., & Lin, H. (2023). Current and lasting effects of affect labeling on late positive potential (LPP) amplitudes elicited by negative events. *Brain and Behavior, 13(7)*, e3065. https://doi.org/10.1002/brb3.3065
8. Torre, J. B., & Lieberman, M. D. (2018). Putting feelings into words: Affect labeling as implicit emotion regulation. *Emotion Review, 10(2)*, 116–124. https://doi.org/10.1177/1754073917742706
9. Yoshimura, S., et al. (2023). Changes in neural activity during the combining affect labeling and reappraisal to negative emotion. *Neuroscience Research, 186*, 1–9. https://doi.org/10.1016/j.neures.2022.10.008
10. Shinpei, Y., et al. (2024). Diminished negative emotion regulation through affect labeling and reappraisal: Insights from functional near infrared spectroscopy on lateral prefrontal cortex activation. *BMC Psychology, 12*, Article 2103. https://doi.org/10.1186/s40359-024-02103-y

Chapter 15: Narrating Your Way to Your Best

1. Appelbaum, L. G., et al. (2023). Synaptic plasticity and mental health: methods, challenges and opportunities. *Neuropsychopharmacology*. https://doi.org/10.1038/s41386-022-01370-w
2. Langille, J. J., & Gallistel, C. R. (2018). The synaptic theory of memory: A historical survey and reconciliation of recent opposition. *Frontiers in Systems Neuroscience*. https://doi.org/10.3389/fnsys.2018.00052
3. Dijkstra, N., et al. (2025). A neural basis for distinguishing imagination from reality. *Neuron*. https://doi.org/10.1016/j.neuron.2025.03.015
4. Ladda, A. M., Lebon, F., & Lotze, M. (2021). Using motor imagery practice for improving motor performance: A review. *Brain and Cognition, 150*, 105705. https://doi.org/10.1016/j.bandc.2021.105705
5. Crum, A. J., & Langer, E. J. (2007). Mind-set matters: Exercise and the placebo effect. *Psychological Science, 18(2)*, 165–171. https://doi.org/10.1111/j.1467-9280.2007.01867.x
6. Riepenhausen, A., Wackerhagen, C., et al. (2022). Positive cognitive reappraisal in stress resilience, mental health, and well-being: A comprehensive systematic review. *Emotion Review*. https://doi.org/10.1177/17540739221114642
7. Stover, A. D., et al. (2024). A meta-analysis of cognitive reappraisal and personal resilience. *Clinical Psychology Review*. https://doi.org/10.1016/j.cpr.2024.102049

Chapter 16: Planning Intentional Recovery

1. Bosch, C., & Sonnentag, S. (2019). Should I take a break? A daily reconstruction study on predicting micro-breaks at work. *International Journal of Stress Management, 26*(4), 378–388.

Chapter 17: Clarifying Your Micro Mission

1. Åsberg, K., Löf, M., & Bendtsen, M. (2025). Setting goals and accepting challenges for behavior change—Analysis of participants' interactions with a digital multiple health behavior intervention: Mixed methods study. *JMIR Human Factors, 12*, Article e66208. https://doi.org/10.2196/66208
2. Putt, M. E., Reese, P. P., Volpp, K. G., Russell, L. B., Loewenstein, G., Yan, J., Barankay, I. (2019). The habit formation trial of behavioral economic interventions to improve statin use and reduce the risk of cardiovascular disease: Rationale, design and methodologies. *Clinical Trials, 16*(4), 399–409. https://doi.org/10.1177/1740774519846852
3. Woolley, K., Giurge, L. M., & Fishbach, A. (2025). Adherence to personal resolutions across time, culture, and goal domains. *Psychological Science*. https://doi.org/10.1177/09567976251350960
4. Dickson, J. M., Hart, A., Fox-Harding, C., & Huntley, C. D. (2023). Adaptive goal processes and underlying motives that sustain mental wellbeing and New Year exercise resolutions. *International Journal of Environmental Research and Public Health, 20*(2), Article 901. https://doi.org/10.3390/ijerph20020901

Chapter 18: Impactful Growth Plan

1. Parke, M., Weinhardt, J. M., Brodsky, A., Tangirala, S., & DeVoe, S. E. (2018). When daily planning improves employee performance: The importance of planning type, engagement, and interruptions. *Journal of Applied Psychology, 103*(4), 339–351. https://doi.org/10.1037/apl0000278
2. Wang, G., Wang, Y., & Gai, X. (2021). A meta-analysis of the effects of mental contrasting with implementation intentions on goal attainment. *Frontiers in Psychology, 12*, Article 565202. https://doi.org/10.3389/fpsyg.2021.565202
3. Trenz, N., & Keith, N. (2024). Promoting new habits at work through implementation intentions. *Journal of Occupational and Organizational Psychology, 97*(4), 1813–1834. https://doi.org/10.1111/joop.12540

4. van Elzelingen, W., van der Plasse, G., van der Werf, Y. D., van Wingen, G. A., & Cools, R. (2022). Striatal dopamine signals are region specific and temporally stable across action-sequence habit formation. *Current Biology*, *32(5)*, 1163–1174.e6. https://doi.org/10.1016/j.cub.2021.12.027
5. Berkman, E. T. (2018). The neuroscience of goals and behavior change. *Consulting Psychology Journal: Practice and Research*, *70(1)*, 28–44. https://doi.org/10.1037/cpb0000094

Chapter 19: Your Environment

1. Carden, L., & Wood, W. (2018). Habit formation and change. *Current Opinion in Behavioral Sciences*, *20*, 117–122. https://doi.org/10.1016/j.cobeha.2017.12.009
2. Yamada, K., & Toda, K. (2023). Habit formation viewed as structural change in the behavioral network. *Communications Biology*, 6, 303. https://doi.org/10.1038/s42003-023-04500-2
3. Patel, D. A., Graupmann, V., & Ferrari, J. R. (2023). Reactance, decisional procrastination, and hesitation: A latent class analysis of clutter behavior. *International Journal of Environmental Research and Public Health*, *20(3)*, Article 2061. https://doi.org/10.3390/ijerph20032061
4. Biedermann, D., Schwarz, P. O., Yau, J., & Drachsler, H. (2023). The effect of social support features via buddies in app-based habit building. *International Journal of Mobile and Blended Learning*.

Acknowledgments

THIS BOOK WAS shaped by years of working alongside people operating in complex, high-pressure environments. Leaders, teams, and professionals across industries trusted us with their challenges and allowed us to experience—up close—what sustainable human performance actually requires when pressure is unavoidable and the stakes are real.

We are deeply grateful to our partners in Fortune 500 organizations, the United States Military, and various Government Agencies who put our methods into practice in the real world. Your willingness to challenge conventional approaches to stress, recovery, and performance helped refine the principles in this book and reinforce a simple truth: stress is not a sign that something is broken. It is part of modern life. What matters is how intentionally we manage stress, energy, and recovery over time.

This work has also been strengthened by the many conversations, moments of reflection, and practical experiments with hundreds of people from all walks of life that occurred far beyond formal programs or presentations. Those experiences shaped not only what we included, but what we deliberately left out.

Finally, this book would not exist without the support of our families. Thank you for your patience, encouragement, and understanding throughout the writing process—and for continually reminding us to live the principles we share here.

And to you, the reader: we hope this work helps you navigate pressure more intentionally, recover more effectively, and sustain performance in the moments that matter most.

About the Authors

Kevin Kachin, PhD, is a renowned human performance specialist and expert in stress recovery and energy management. With a doctorate in Clinical Psychology from Penn State University, Dr. Kachin has dedicated his career to helping individuals, leaders, and organizations thrive under pressure by harnessing science-backed strategies to manage stress and optimize performance.

He is Co-Founder and Chief Strategy Officer at Impact Human Performance. He has coached executives, athletes, and teams on managing stress more effectively and recovering effectively from the never-ending demands of modern life. Drawing from years of research and practical application in clinical and corporate settings, his approach emphasizes working with the body's natural responses rather than against them. He lives in West Palm Beach, Florida.

Nick Propper has held senior leadership roles in the Professional Services Industry during a 20+ year career spanning both pan-European and Global responsibilities.

He is the Co-Founder and Chief Executive Officer of Impact Human Performance, where he works with leaders and teams operating in some of the most demanding environments in the world. His work focuses on helping people sustain high performance under immense pressure by moving beyond short-term fixes and toward practical, evidence-informed approaches that enable people to perform well, recover intentionally, and remain effective over the long term. He lives in Westport, Connecticut.

Index

Numerics
1-3-2 technique, 132
The 1% Rule, 78–79

A
achievement neurotransmitter, 186
action
    goal-oriented, 186
    growth plan, xv, 185–187
    Stressed Self in, 23–32
acute stressors, 151–152
    resilient stress response,
        158–162
adrenaline rises, 9, 162
"All roads lead to recovery," 74–76
ambiguity, 34
American Journal of Preventive Medicine, 94
amygdala, 9, 159, 163
ATP production, 114, 117
awareness
    Best Self. *See* Best Self
    emotional labeling, 158–163
    emotional regulation, 72–73
    stress, 23
        experience of, 24–25
        responses, 30–32
        Stressed Self. *See* Stressed Self
        warning signs, 25–30

B
balance
    breathing. *See* breathing
    fluid, 117
    hydration. *See* hydration
Balanced Brain Breathing, 124, 126–131
barriers
    Best Self, 53–56
    movement, 109–110
bedtime routine, 140
behaviors
    recovery strategies, 90–91
    responding, 56
beliefs, stories, 166–168
Best Case, 185
    growth plan, 185–187
Best Self, ix–x, xiv, xv, xvi, 4, 12, 19–21, 90,
        198. *See also* Stressed Self
    barriers, 53
        intervene and change course, 56
        responding vs reacting, 54–55
    beliefs, 166–167
    chronic stressor, 152–153
    creating environments, 49–51
    cutting off connection, 44
    defining, 45–47
    emotional regulation. *See* emotional,
        regulation

Best Self (*continued*)
- environment cues, 176, 191–194
- exercises, 47–52
- expectations, 52
- flexible focus, 30
- growth plan, 185–187
- honesty, 171–172
- human energy system, 165
- identity, 166–168
- perspective, shifting, 169, 175
- process, 43–44
- recovery. *See* intentional recovery
- rewriting the narration, 175–176
- self-awareness, 48–49
- showing up, 167
- thoughts, 165–166, 168–169

Big 6 Lymph Reset, 142–145
body
- alarm system, 3
- cross-lateral movements, 104–108
- detoxification process, 140–141
- lack of movement, 93–94
- prolonged sitting, 93–94
- for quality sleep, 140
- safety signal, 148

brain
- breathing. *See* breathing
- danger mode, 91
- safety signal, 123
- sleeping. *See* sleeping
- waves, 105

brain-based activities, 114
brainstorm, 155
breathing
- beyond stress, 132–133
- conscious, 132–133
- consequences of chronic, 125–126
- incorporating, 133–134
- inhale and exhale, 131–132
- intentional, 123
- practices, 127–128, 131
- unconscious restrictive, 124–125

C
calf-raising movement, 100–104
cellular energy production, 124
challenges, hydration, 120–122
chronic
- dehydration, 114
- sleep deprivation, 136
- stress, xi, 3, 16–22
  - mode, signs, 21–22
- stressors, 151–152
  - managing, 152–153
  - VIP model, 154–155
- stress physiology, 6, 10–11
- workplace stress, xii, 93, 152–153

classical conditioning, 191
classic stress response, 27
close loop, 52
cognitive
- stimulation, 139
- stress, 97

competence model, 36
connection, human attention, 44, 189
conscious breathing, 132–133
consistent movement, 96–98
constant demands, 53
corpus callosum, 104, 126
cortisol, 9, 106
cross-lateral movement, 104–108, 120
Crum, Alia, 168
"cutting off" human connection, 44

D
danger signal, 151
dehydration
- factors, minimizing, 120
- hydration and, 114–116

detoxification process, 140–141
- consequences of, 141–145
- gratitude practice, 145–146

distractions, 53
distress (negative), 13–14
drainage, lymphatic, 142–145, 148

E
electrolyte-rich foods, 115–118, 120
emotional
- content, 139
- labeling, 158–163
- labor, 34
- regulation, 4, 18, 33–35, 57
  - awareness, 72–74
  - conscious breathing, 132
  - high performance, 59–60
  - intentional recovery, 68–71, 74–76
  - model for, 58–59, 70
  - stress response, 61–64
- stress signs, 25, 28, 29

energy
- high, 94
- hydration. *See* hydration

levels, maintains, 96
in and out, 81, 84
environments
creating, Best Self, 49–51
cues, 191–194
repetition, rewiring through, 194
shaping, 172, 176
stress, 10, 12
Epictetus (Stoic philosopher), 149
eustress (positive), 13–14
exhale and inhale breathing, 131–132
experiencing
forced recovery, 64–68
frustration, 49
stress, 24–25, 31
eye stretch, 106–107

F
fascia (tight connective tissue), 106, 118–119
fascial maneuvers routine, 108
feelings
changing, 89, 91
little off, 26
responding, 56
fiber (C-tactile), 105
fifteen-minute recovery ideas, 181
"fight-or-flight" response (danger signal), 106
five-minute recovery ideas, 181
fluid
balance, 117
loss, 120
focus, flexible, 30
foods, water/mineral-rich, 116–118
foot pumps, 101
forced recovery, 4, 20
emotional state, 64–68
Frankl, Viktor, 15, 39
frustration, experiences of, 49

G
glymphatic system, 135
goal-oriented action, 186
gratitude practice, 145–148
growth-based emotional regulation, 58–59
growth plan, 175, 185–186
environment, 194
impactful, 187

H
"habit stacking," 121–122
hand squeeze and release, 102
"hard pivots," 130
Harvard University, 168
healthy breathing, 124–125
high
energy, 94
survival state, 62–63
performance, 4, 59–60
homeostasis, line of, 81–83
homework assignment, 145
hormones, stress, 9, 17
human connection
attention, 189
"cutting off," 44
human energy
battery, 78–79
system, 54, 57–58, 83–84, 90, 165
"hungry lions" modern, 3, 9–10
hydration
challenges, 120–122
and dehydration, 114–116
and mineralization, 113, 121
and movement, 118–119
practical strategies, 119–120
water-rich foods, 116–118
hyper-distraction, 29–30
hyper-focus, 29–30
hyperventilation, 125

I
identity-level stories, 166–168, 171–173
impactful growth plan, 187
Impact Human Performance (IHP), xii–xiii, xvi, 90, 151
inactivity, long stretches of, 99–100
inhale and exhale breathing, 131–132
injury modification, 102
integrating movement, 107–112
intellectual foundation, 166
intensity, stressor(s), 154–155, 157
intentional breathing, 123
intentional recovery, 4, 20, 22, 68–71, 74–76, 89
behavioral suggestions, 90–91
menu with options, 181–182
micro-breaks, 179
micro-recovery ideas, 180–181
moments of, 77
The 1% Rule, 78–79
homeostasis, line of, 81–82
human energy battery, 78–79
oscillation framework, 83–84
patterns, 80–83

intentional recovery (*continued*)
prioritizing, 79
recognizing the signs, 79–80
rest, 22
internal warning signs, 78
interpretation, 55, 162
and regulation, 12

L
Levine, James (Dr.), 93
long-term stress, 18–19
loops, close and open, 52
lymphatic drainage system, 97, 141–145, 148
lymph nodes and vessels, 141

M
managing stress, 22
Mayo Clinic, 93
meditation, 191–192
mental stress signs, 25, 28–30
micro-breaks, 179
micro danger signals, 11, 15
micro mission, 176, 182
clarifying, 183–184
goals, 185–186
micro-recovery ideas, 180–181
mind
quality sleep, 140
slows down, 106
mineral-rich foods, 113, 117–118, 120
modern-day lions, 10
movement, regulate stress
benefits of, 94
calf-raising, 100–104
consistent, 96–98, 105
cross-lateral, 104–108
hydration and, 118–119
lack of, 93
levels of, 95–96
physical activity, 94
routine, integrating, 107–112
tracking, 98–100

N
Nadi Shodhana, 126
narrating stories
beliefs, 166–167
changing, 175
honesty, 171–175
human energy system, 165
identity, aligned, 166, 168
rewriting the, 175–176
thoughts, 166, 168–169
negative (distress), 13–14
nervous system, 11, 15, 21
breathing
parasympathetic and sympathetic, 10, 12, 127
chronic stress, 17–18, 20
neural plasticity, 136
neurological repair and reset, 136
neurotransmitter function, 114
neutral stimulus, 191
Nickelston, Perry (Dr.), 142

O
OCR. *See* oculocardiac reflex
oculocardiac reflex (OCR), 106
one-minute recovery ideas, 180–181
open loops, 52
opportunities, adding movement, 108–109
optimization, sleep, 136–140
oscillation, pattern, 83–84
overhydration, 117
overstimulation, 53
oxygen, 125–126, 132

P
parasympathetic nervous system (safety signal), 10, 20, 123
breathing, 127
self hug activates, 105–106
Pardoe, T. Earl, 35
passive repetition, 31, 48
pattern stress recovery, 80–81
pavlovian conditioning, 191
perception, stressor(s), 154–155, 157
performance, high, 4, 59–60
personal
recovery, 89
warning signs, 5
perspective, shifting, 169, 175
physical
activity, patterns of, 94–100
stress signs, 25, 28, 29
symptoms, 19
physiology
perspective, 169
regulation movements, 94
stress, 10, 29
positive (eustress), 13–14
practical strategies, hydration, 119–120

pranayama. *See* Nadi Shodhana
predictive breathwork, 129
prioritize recovery, 79
proactive planning, 158
productivity, 89
prolonged sitting, 93, 97–98

Q
quadrants, emotional regulation model, 59, 72–73

R
reacting stress, 158
  emotional and logical state, 159–160
  vs responding, 38–42, 54–56
real-time response management, 15
recognizing
  Stressed Self. *See* Stressed Self, recognizing
recovery
  forced, 64–68
  intentional, 4, 68–71, 89
    behavioral suggestions, 90–91
    menu with options, 181–182
    micro-breaks, 179
    micro-recovery ideas, 180–181
  sleeping and, 141–142
  stress pattern, 80–81
reflection activity, stress, 37–38
regular movement
  benefits of, 96
  incorporating, 100
regulation, 12
  emotional, 4, 18, 33–35, 57
  interpretation and, 12
  model for, 58–59
repetition
  passive, 48
  rewiring through, 194
resilient stress response, 158–162
resistance arises, stress, 23–24
responding vs reacting stress, 54–56
responses
  stress, 7–9, 53
    classic, 27
    reacting to, 38–42
    resilient, 158–162
  stressors, managing, 149–150
rest, intentional, 22
restrictive breathing
  consequences of chronic, 125–126
  unconscious, 124–125
retrospective scorecard, 14
reverse toe tap, 107–108
ripple effects, xi, 154
rotational movements, 120
routine
  balanced brain breathing, 128
  bedtime, 140
  effective ways movement, 107–112
  for hydration, 121
  sleep. *See* sleeping

S
safety signal, 106, 123
  sleeping. *See* sleeping
second heart, 100–104
self hug, 105–106
self-management literature, 89
shallow breathing
  consequences of chronic, 125–126
  unconscious, 124–125
signs, stress warning, 25–30, 79–80
sitting
  extended periods, 93
  new smoking, 93
  prolonged, 93
sleeping
  bedtime routine, 140
  Big 6 Lymph Reset, 142–145
  deprivation, 170–171
  lymphatic system, 141–142
  optimization, 136–140
  practicing gratitude, 145
  purpose of, 135–136
  and recovery, 141–142
  trouble, 18–19
sodium-potassium pump, 117
spleen, 141
squeezing and releasing, hands, 102
stimulation
  cognitive, 139
  lymph, 142
stories. *See* narrating stories
strategies
  hydration, 119–120
  movement. *See* movement, regulate stress
  stressors, managing, 151–155
stress (internal reaction), 3
  breathing. *See* breathing
  chronic, 3, 16–22
  invisible, 4
  movement. *See* movement, regulate stress

stress (*continued*)
physiology of, 10–12
proper hydration, 120–121
recovery pattern, 80–81
responses, 4, 7–9, 53, 61–64, 150–151
science of, 13–16
understanding, 5–7
vs stressors, 7–9
warning signs, xv, 4, 25–30, 79–80
Stressed Self, ix, xiv, xv, xvi, 12–16, 18, 20, 22, 175, 197–198. *See also* Best Self
competence model, 36
emotional regulation, 33–35, 57
reacting, 56
to responding, 38–42
recognizing, 4, 23–24
experience of, 24–25
responses, 30–32
warning signs, 25–32
reflection activity, 37–38
Stressed Selves, 33, 45
environments and, 51
warning signs, 48
stress-free life, 22
stressors (the external triggers), 3
chronic stress, 19
managing, 149–150
acute, 151–152
resilient stress response, 158–162
chronic, 151–153
VIP model, 153–157
responses, 149–150
stress vs, 7–9
Stress Warning Signs Post-Its, 31
stretching, eye, 106–107
structured water, 118
survival-based emotional regulation, 58–59
survival mode, xi, 61–64
sympathetic nervous system, 10
breathing, 127
synapses, 166

T
thirst, dehydration, 114
thoughts, 166
changing, 89, 91
power of, 168–169
responding, 56
thymus, 141
tight connective tissue (fascia), 106
tipping point, 18–21
toe tap, reverse, 107–108
Tolle, Eckhart, 35–36
tracking movement, 98–100
two-minute breathing, 83

U
UCLA, 158
unconscious restrictive breathing, 124–125
unique stress responses, 5–7

V
vagus nerve, 107
VIP model, 153–157
volume, stressor(s), 154–155, 157

W
warning signs
internal, 78
personal, 5–7
stress, xv, 4, 5, 14, 15, 25–30
water
drinking enough, 113–114
structured, 118
water-rich foods, 116–117, 119, 121
wind-down practice, 136, 139
workplace
chronic stressor, 152–153
stress-related issues, xii, 93
worst case scenarios, 186

Y
yogic practices, 126